A Form and Style Manual for Lawyers

Ian Gallacher

ASSSISTANT PROFESSOR OF LAW &
DIRECTOR OF LEGAL RESEARCH AND WRITING
SYRACUSE UNIVERSITY COLLEGE OF LAW

CAROLINA ACADEMIC PRESS
Durham, North Carolina

Library of Congress Cataloging-in-Publication Data

Gallacher, Ian, 1956-
A form and style manual for lawyers / by Ian Gallacher.
   p. cm.
ISBN 1-59460-096-1 (alk. paper)
1. Legal composition.   I. Title.
KF250.G35 2005
808'.06634--dc22   2005019842

CAROLINA ACADEMIC PRESS
700 Kent Street
Durham, North Carolina 27701
Telephone (919) 489-7486
Fax (919) 493-5668
www.cap-press.com

Printed in the United States of America
Cover Design: Erin M. Ehman

A Form and Style Manual
for Lawyers

To Julie, who makes our garden grow

Contents

Acknowledgments

No book is written by one person alone: Writing is a collaborative enterprise. Yet trying to thank everyone who has helped me develop the thoughts and ideas expressed here would require another book. And plowing though a list of names is rarely an enjoyable task for a reader.

Nevertheless, there are some people to whom I am so indebted that I must acknowledge them here. The Honorable Frederic N. Smalkin, Shannon Hanson, Pat Taves, Jan Brodie, Charles Goodell, Richard Barnes, Thomas Waxter, Kelly Hughes-Iverson, Teri Leonovich, Lauren Lacy, Shannon Madden Marshall, Nikki Nesbit, Michael McWilliams, Martin Hudson, William Nealon, Robert Wilzcek, Scott Fisher, James Comodeca, Gina Saelinger, Pamela White, and Heather McCabe—all in their own ways—helped me to develop as a legal writer. Lee Titus Elliott showed me how to edit my work. Eric Easton, Amy Dillard, Jeremy Mullem, and Nancy Modesitt showed me how to be a more effective teacher. And I wouldn't be a teacher at all without the faith and confidence of Penny Pether. Thanks also to my students at the Washington College of Law and Syracuse University College of Law, especially Cindy Hamra, Sun Hee Chim, Amy Raaf, Katherine Ellis, Jarrett Perlow, and Andrea Moore Stover. Thanks also to my two Deans—Claudio Grossman and Hannah Arterian—for their support, and to my colleagues at the Syracuse University College of Law—Elizabeth August, Joe Dole, Kate Dole, Elton Fukumoto, Jill Paquette, Lucille Rignanese, and Richard Risman—for their dedication and hard work.

No student could ever have had a better teacher than Jean Redman, and no son could have had better parents than Henry Gallacher and Joan Upton-Holder. Thanks, finally, to Julia McKinstry, who makes everything worthwhile and to whom, as always, this book is dedicated.

Ian Gallacher
Marcellus, New York
April, 2005

A Form and Style Manual
for Lawyers

Chapter 1

Introduction

This manual is designed to give you some very basic information about the writing process and some of the more technical aspects of writing. It will walk you through the steps you can take to produce acceptable, generic, and professional legal documents of the kind most often used in litigation. Its only purpose is to help you generate documents that look and sound as if they were written by a lawyer. This manual won't tell you how to write or think like a lawyer; it won't tell you how to research the law; it won't tell you how to cite a case or statute; and it won't tell you how to get an A in your legal writing and research class.

Form and style seems like a modest subject, but experience as a lawyer and law teacher has shown me that finding and assimilating the information contained in this book can be difficult for law students and new lawyers. And it is important information: a brilliant analysis ungrammatically written or poorly punctuated will carry less weight than the same analysis with no mistakes, and while there should be nothing magical about the way a document looks, readers will tend to discount the analysis in a memorandum or brief if it isn't organized in a standard and visually appealing manner. Furthermore, a document not formatted according to court requirements may not even make it to a judge's desk if the clerk's office rejects it.

This manual isn't written in the formal style you should employ when writing an interoffice memorandum or a brief for filing in court. In fact, your language shouldn't be this relaxed in most of what you write as a lawyer. Your writing style should change with the context of your writing. Here, I'm not writing a brief; I'm writing a book on document formatting, grammar, and punctuation, three topics about which most people don't read for enjoyment. So I've adopted a more relaxed writing style to try to keep you interested in and engaged with the subject. The moral here is to follow the suggestions contained in this manual, not to write in the style in which these suggestions are made.

This isn't a book you'll read all the way through in one sitting. You'll find the material more helpful if you dip into it when you're confronted with a problem about drafting or when you have a question about grammar or punctuation. In addition, you should annotate the text if you're given contradictory advice by your teachers or supervisors or by court requirements: the book contains very few rules, only suggestions you should feel free to ignore—especially if they conflict with the rhetorical and stylistic principles expected by your reader. One of the few absolute rules in writing is that the reader is always right.

All the writing suggestions in this book are generic: they are not tailored for any specific jurisdiction or law firm. Procedures regarding form and style may well be carried out differently in your jurisdiction and therefore jurisdictional rules or local practices will always trump any stylistic and rhetorical principles I've given here. Again, annotate the stylistic rules and practices in the text that differ from those of your own locality and you'll have a jurisdiction-specific reference that's more helpful than anything I've written.

This manual is intended to lower your stress level so that you can concentrate on the important work you do, both as law students and as lawyers. I hope it succeeds in this goal.

Chapter 2

Before You Begin

The process of writing a legal document begins well before you start putting pen to paper or, in this electronic age, fingers to keyboard. There are several crucial steps you should take before you start placing words onto the paper or screen, without which your finished work is doomed. Though simple, these steps are vital to your success as a legal writer.

Experience teaches that not all law students or lawyers are as familiar with these steps as they could be. If you understand all about time management, you needn't spend long reading this chapter. But be careful that you know this material as well as you think you do, because overconfidence in knowing the fundamentals can be harmful to your development as a writer. If you ask successful lawyers about the most important thing you should have when starting to practice law, they'll most likely emphasize that you should have your own calendaring system—either paper or electronic—with a method for reminding you about critical stages in your work.

A. Establish Your Ultimate Deadline

The first step in any writing project—before you start formulating issues or researching the law—is to determine when you must submit the finished work. As a law student, you are usually given very specific deadlines: you will be told that a particular project must be submitted by a certain time on a certain date. You should understand that these are firm deadlines: 9:00 a.m. on Monday November 1, for example, does not mean 9:01 a.m. on Monday November 1. Work submitted late will be treated accordingly, no matter how late it is.

In fact, students who come to law school directly from undergraduate schools are sometimes surprised that law school deadlines are as firm as they are, apparently believing that a deadline is just the opening gambit in a negotiation. (Concerning the deadline requirement, law school tracks the real world of lawyering, but the requirement is not always rigidly enforced. In law school, it may be possible to get an extension from a sympathetic teacher.)

But whatever your experience may have been as a law student, deadlines in law practice will be strictly enforced. If you're told on Friday at 4:00 p.m. that a partner expects to see a draft of a memo or brief on Monday at 9:00 a.m., that's when the partner expects to see it. Explaining that you have already made plans for the weekend will not help you if you don't get the work done, nor will your failure to find a law to help you develop a convincing theory, nor will your accurate perception that your partner's "unreasonable" expectations aren't fair. Lawyers are expected to produce professional work, in response to the assignment given them and at the specified time.

Perhaps producing quality work delivered by a strict deadline is unreasonable, and perhaps this expectation is what gives some law firms the reputation of being "sweat shops" (although anyone who knows of conditions in real sweat shops should be ashamed to use that term to describe the way young lawyers are treated). But the expectation of producing quality work delivered on time is the culture in law practice and you should get used to it in law school. Your life as a practicing lawyer will be easier if you know what to expect.

i. Do Your Own Calendaring

In practice, many lawyers will hand over the responsibility of determining filing deadlines to secretaries or paralegals. This is a bad idea for at least three reasons. First, these deadlines are established by court rules—either by the rules of civil procedure for your jurisdiction or by the local rules of the court where a case is filed—and interpreting these rules is something lawyers, not secretaries or paralegals, are trained to do. Second, courts are unlikely to have sympathy for a highly paid lawyer's excuse that interpreting the court's rules of procedure is a task better suited to a secretary and that any mistakes are therefore the secretary's fault. Third, even if the court deems the lawyer's failure to honor a deadline to be "excusable neglect," it's unlikely that the client whose case was jeopardized, or the insurance company whose assets were placed in peril by the lawyer's potential malpractice, will be so understanding. Consequently, lawyers should become familiar with the filing deadlines of each court in which they practice and should keep their own calendars of events.

So buy a calendar, or use your computer software's electronic calendaring system, and track your own deadlines. If your law firm has a calendaring system, then your own record will be a shadow calendar, but keep it yourself: don't delegate this task to others. And check your calendar daily to see what deadlines are approaching and when. Get used to doing this in law school and it'll become such an ingrained habit that you'll never have to worry about missing a crucial date.

ii. Anticipate Technical Problems

As you become more experienced, you must (and will) develop a sensitivity to the ultimate deadline for each project—often referred to as the "drop dead" deadline in the unfortunate jargon lawyers use. This means you must consider the possibility of a technical problem while trying to get your document in final form to be submitted.

We all know the frustration of the computer freezing up, or the printer jamming, or the other glitches that can happen to your computer system, usually as you're trying to print out a finished work for submission. Unfortunately, time doesn't freeze along with your hard drive. So any technological glitches you experience probably won't be acceptable as excuses for late filing in law school, and they almost certainly won't be acceptable as excuses when you're in practice. This policy may seem harsh, but it's important for you to get into the habit of protecting yourself from these potential problems: back up your work regularly; save your drafts and store them on disk as well as on your hard drive; print and store unmarked copies of your drafts. Indeed, there are many steps you can take to minimize problems when they occur. At the very least, they'll support your argument for an extension; more important, developing a strong factual record in support of your position is a skill you'll need throughout your legal career.

B. Establish Your Intermediate Deadlines

The ultimate deadline is only the last in a series of deadlines, and it's the only one you're given. You must establish the other, intermediate deadlines yourself, based on your work habits and your personal circumstances. Between the two principal pillars of a project—getting the assignment and submitting the finished project—there are at least ten of these intermediate deadlines to schedule:

- Develop a research strategy
- Begin research
- End research
- Prepare an outline
- Begin writing
- End writing
- Begin editing
- End editing
- Print final draft
- Proofread final draft

It might seem that some of these intermediate deadlines aren't particularly significant and that there's no need to structure your time this methodically. But be careful. Time has a way of slipping away from you.

Suppose, for example, that you are given a law school writing project to complete in four weeks. During that time, you have a midterm exam scheduled in one of your classes and an out-of-state wedding you're planning to attend over a weekend. You will likely spend some time preparing for the exam, and you will likely do little work on the Friday, Saturday, and Sunday of the wedding weekend. Factor in the understandable desire not to spend every weekend working on your writing project, your other class preparation, and your appropriate attempts to maintain a balance between law school and the rest of your life, and you will see that you have substantially less than the four weeks you initially thought you had in which to complete the assignment.

i. Develop a Schedule

One way to gain at least a semblance of control over this process is to develop a schedule by deciding how long you will need to accomplish each of the intermediate steps in the drafting of a document, working backwards from the ultimate deadline. So, in the example I've set out below, let's assume you've been given a project on October 1 and your ultimate deadline is 9:00 a.m. on November 1. Your intermediate deadlines might look like this:

- **Proofread final draft**: October 31. You will need to set at least some time aside for the possibility that you will find mistakes that require correction during the final proofreading process. Also, you must anticipate the possibility that your computer or printer will malfunction.

- **Print out final draft**: October 30. You should perform your final proofreading fresh so that you'll be likely to catch mistakes rather than glide over them. To do this, you'll need at least one night's sleep between the last time you worked on the document and the proofreading itself. And printing it out the day before will allow you at least a day if some complete disaster should befall your computer and you have to retype the whole document.

- **End editing:** October 30.

- **Begin editing:** October 23. Editing is, or should be, a big job. You should be willing to make extensive changes in your document, including moving sections around, jettisoning sections that don't work, and redrafting sections to make them more compelling. You might even discover the need to do more research and incorporate that research into an already existing section or a new section you're going to draft. We'll talk more about editing later in this manual.

- **End writing:** October 21. Just as you should begin your final proofreading fresh, so you should begin editing after taking a short break from the project. During that time you'll be thinking about what you've written, what went right, and what you're not satisfied with. Giving yourself a couple of days to think about these matters before coming back to your work should allow you to edit more effectively and efficiently.

- **Begin writing:** October 13. Writing is a difficult task, and it's a tiring process if it's to be done correctly. Unless you're a workaholic, you won't be able to write legal analysis for large chunks of time. Rather, you'll work in short segments, two or three times a day. That's fine, but you'll need to make sure you have enough time to get the document drafted without shortchanging the remainder of the writing process.

- **Prepare an outline:** October 12. This is an important part of the process and you should take it seriously. Once you've outlined what it is you're going to write, give yourself a little time to reflect on your outline before actually starting to write. You may discover that you've left out a crucial part of the analysis or that you can reorder your work a little to make it more coherent.

- **End research**: October 12. There's no reason to delay outlining what you're going to write once you've completed your research, so plan to outline as the last step in your research process. You'll likely have been thinking about what you're going to say and how you're going to say it anyway, so you might as well get your main points on paper right away. Besides, outlining often shows gaps in your research you'll need to plug before writing the analysis.

- **Begin research**: October 2. Research is the least familiar task you will face during the legal-writing process, at least initially, so you should budget a lot of time to accomplish it. In addition, just as with writing, you likely won't research in large chunks of time, so you should give yourself enough time to be sure you've covered *all* aspects of your research.

- **Develop a research strategy**: October 1. This is the date you get the assignment, and the first thing you should do after determining your ultimate turn-in date is to think about the question you've been asked to answer and how you're going to go about answering it. You should mull the project over and think about how best to research the issues. You may even want to spend some time researching your research strategy (rereading portions of your research textbook, for example, in order to confirm or disprove some of your thoughts about research strategy). Giving yourself some time to reflect on your decisions before beginning the research itself gives you the chance to reconsider portions of your research plan.

As you can see, this schedule gives you no time for outside commitments like the midterm exam or the wedding. These commitments will reduce the amount of time you have to accomplish the tasks necessary to turn in a well-researched and well-written piece of work by the deadline. But by setting dates on which these intermediate tasks should be completed, you can adjust your schedule to make certain you won't compress the researching and writing into the weekend immediately before the submission deadline and thereby virtually ensure your work won't have received the thorough—and necessary—editing and proofreading.

ii. Allow Enough Time for the Writing Process

Remember that the process of legal writing doesn't break down neatly into a research phase and a writing phase as the above hypothetical plan may seem to indicate. Writing is, or should be, a dynamic process. Once you begin to write, you'll discover that you need to do more research into certain areas, and you'll write down some preliminary thoughts about your analysis while you're still researching. That's fine. It's the way almost every writer of legal documents works, so you shouldn't straitjacket yourself just because the way you want to work doesn't fit neatly into the schedule you've constructed. Use your intermediate-deadline schedule as an outline for finishing your writing project rather than as a fixed blueprint. But try to stay as close to your schedule as you can, given the inevitable changes that will occur.

In the chaotic world of law practice, making a schedule like the above may seem unrealistic. No sooner will you have started on the first step in your writing plan than someone will call you up to do another project, and suddenly you'll find that several days have gone by and you haven't even started your research yet. No amount of organization can prevent this from happening, of course, but creating a written schedule for each major writing project can still be beneficial. Even if events knock you off track, the schedule will remind you of where you are in the project, of what you have done, and of what you still have to do. Also it will be a more accurate record than your memory. Besides, if you keep getting interruptions and the project is coming due, you can show your schedule to the partner who wants you to work on yet another assignment. A written document showing how much time you have left to spend on a current project will usually be more persuasive than your spoken excuses about the weight of your workload.

iii. Allow Time for Your Work to Be Reviewed

If your written work will be reviewed by other lawyers and especially if a client wants to see what will be filed before the work is sent out, you must factor such delays into your schedule. If a lawyer reviews your work, you should know that the more senior a lawyer becomes, the more that lawyer will forget how long it takes to incorporate edits into a document, so you should take this into account when you create your schedule. If, for example, you have a document one page short of a court's page limit and your partner adds three pages of edits at lunchtime on the day the document is due, you will have difficulty getting the document prepared and filed in time. Inevitably, the fault will be yours, not the partner's.

There are some steps you can take to protect yourself against this problem. First, always try to leave some space in the document. In the world of law practice, "to edit" often means "to add," so leave two or three pages for other lawyers to fill. Second, do not tell lawyers who ask for the filing date of a document the actual filing date, unless you have no choice. Rather, tell them when you need the document back so you can incorporate their changes. Don't lie; just answer the question they should have asked. Third, make sure that all other tasks related to the filing have been done. If you're working on a memorandum in support of a motion, make sure that the motion itself has been completed and copied. Also make sure that any accompanying letter has been written, that a check for the filing fee (if necessary) has been prepared, and that any other task not contingent on someone else's approval has been done. This way you can clear time to incorporate the edits, finalize the document, and get it filed by the deadline.

C. Outlining Your Writing

Outlining your work is one of the most important steps you can take to be certain you will generate a coherent, easy-to-read piece of legal writing. If you are already comfortable with the concept of outlining and are familiar with a system of outlining that works consistently for you, congratulations! But you should read this section anyway, just in case it gives you some new ideas. If you haven't used a system of outlining, you'll have to learn one now: the work you will do in law school and as a lawyer is too complicated to organize in your head, and incoherence will doom good research and writing.

You may think that outlining is a waste of time, an unnecessary preliminary step before the real work is done. But this is a short-sighted view. Outlining your work will save you time when you look at your draft and realize that some information would be better grouped with information at the beginning of your memo rather than halfway through, that other ideas you had about the subject would be better left out of this particular piece of work, and so on. Taking time before you begin to write to think about where information should go, what it should precede, and what it should follow will be time well spent.

I know of two outlining systems, each of which has advantages and disadvantages. The system you use can be one of these, a combination of both, or a system entirely different. What matters most is that you have an effective way of organizing your material before beginning the drafting process.

i. The Traditional Outlining Method

The traditional outlining method is familiar to almost everyone. You start with the Roman numeral I[1] and write down your first point. For each subsidiary portion of that point (or supporting argument), you indent one tab stop and write down a summary of that point after a capital A. For each argument supporting A, you indent another tab stop and use an Arabic numeral (1, 2, 3, and so on) before writing a summary of that point. For each subordinate point under the Arabic numeral, indent another tab stop and start the process again with a lowercase letter, and if that point has subordinate points under it, indent yet another tab stop and list each of them beside a lowercase Roman numeral.

This process is continued until all arguments under I are exhausted. Then you begin the second principal point (II) and keep following the same organizational hierarchy until your complete argument is mapped out.

A simple argument in the traditional outline format might look like this:

    I.   Structure of Class Certification Process
        A. Class representative must be member of class
        B. Class representative must sue or be sued
        C. Filing of class action complaint
            1. relationship between class members and counsel
            2. tolling of statute of limitations?
        D. Rule 23(a) requirements
            1. numerosity
            2. commonality
            3. typicality
            4. adequacy

---

1. I start outlines with I, then A, then 1, then a, then i. Others start with A, but that method loses one level of subordination.

E. Rule 23(b) requirements
   1. (b)(1)(A) classes
   2. (b)(1)(B) classes
   3. (b)(2) classes
   4. (b)(3) classes
       a. class notice
       b. requirements of a (b)(3) class
           i.   predominance
           ii. superiority

Of course, a second section—marked II—will follow, and so on until the analysis is complete.

This is the type of outline your word-processing software will help you prepare. It's very linear in format, and that's one of its strengths: it shows you the order in which your arguments fall and allows you to see if they're grouped in a logical and coherent fashion.

But this linear organization is also one of the traditional format's greatest weaknesses: it tends to stifle creativity. Most of us are inclined to reproach ourselves when we make what we perceive as a "mistake," so when we're outlining in the traditional format, we want to be sure to get the information down in the "correct" order. This way of thinking is, of course, illogical: we're writing the outline in order to decide what the "correct" order is, but there is no "correct" order until after the outlining process is completed. Nevertheless, that fact doesn't stop us from pondering carefully where each entry should go in the structure. If we discover that we've missed a prong of the argument, frequently we'll start again, this time adding the G we forgot in our last outline. This stop-and-go process takes time and cramps our creative thinking exactly when we should be encouraging it to assert itself.

To prevent this restrictive self-editing process many of us inflict on ourselves, there's another, nontraditional outlining method. This method is not my invention, and it has many names, depending on who is writing about it. I'll use the name I first heard applied to it— "branching."

ii. The "Branching" Method

At first, the branching method of outline generation looks un-helpful for lawyers—too much emphasis on free-form thinking and not enough on structure or organization. But that's the value of this method: it keeps you from worrying about structure and allows you to put down ideas more freely. (If the absence of structural support bothers you, don't worry: you can insert a missing point or delete an unnecessary point later.)

Here's how branching works. First, take a blank sheet of paper (lined paper is okay, although the technique works best with un-lined paper). In the center, write down the principal issue under consideration and draw a circle around it. Now draw branches (lines) coming out of that central issue, and then write down what each line represents. These lines can—and should—have their own branches, each with its own short label.

The goal here is to write as much as possible and think (con-sciously, at least) as little as possible, so put down whatever ideas come into your head, whether or not they make sense. If you're writing down one thought and realize you need another line for your present idea to make sense, don't worry: finish up what you're writing, draw another branch, and then set down your most recent thought. There's no order to these branches, so one idea need not follow another on a preceding line when logically the order should be reversed.

Try not to read what you've already written. If you can't remem-ber whether you've already put something down, put it down again. This is not the time to edit. Keep going until you've exhausted all your ideas. Then put your outline away for some period of time—at least an hour, better, a day.

When you come back to your outline, you can take one of two steps. If you think there may be more ideas in you, try to add issues to each of your branches. If you're convinced that you can't add any more, turn your outline into a linear, or traditional, one. You may find that this process stimulates you into thinking of additional arguments you'll need to include, or connections you'll need to make, so that your argument is logical and coherent. Even if you don't discover additional arguments or connections, you'll be generating the outline necessary to start drafting your document. It's during this outlining process that you can review your ideas, discard those that, upon further review, appear not to help or advance your argument, and structure the rest into a logical and coherent whole. But remember: don't be critical of your ideas until this point.

A sample branch outline appears on the page opposite.

Even if the branch outlining process seems odd to you, try it once to see if it helps you generate some ideas. Remember that the goal of branch outlining is to remove the self-editing and critical faculties we all possess and to get ideas down on paper—no matter how unrelated these ideas may at first appear. You never know when you'll get some flash of insight.

D. Multiple Drafts

You'll have noticed in the hypothetical schedule I set out earlier in this chapter that I've given a date for the final draft to be completed. The date assumes that there will be intermediate drafts of the document you're writing before the final draft is finished.

Even if you've had success as an undergraduate writing only one draft of a document, you should get out of that habit when you start to write legal documents. The concepts you're working with are too complicated to be reduced to written form, then analyzed, and finally resolved, in just one draft. Later perhaps, some of your simpler documents you can write adequately in one draft. Almost everything you write, though—and certainly any document you file with a court— should go through at least two drafts, and usually many more. If you are a conscientious writer, the necessity of multiple drafts will not change, no matter how senior a lawyer you will become.

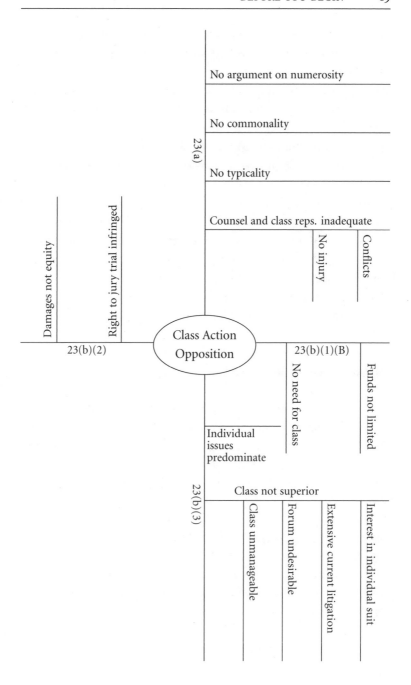

You will probably need to organize your material in your mind, then organize it in some form of outline, then get it down onto the page before you can know the direction your document is taking. You'll probably (although not certainly) know the basic elements, like the final outcome. But you may find once you've written a draft that the path you'd expected to take to that outcome hasn't worked as well as you'd thought, and that another path—one which hadn't occurred to you during your research phase—now looks like a more promising approach.

When this happens, you need to be sensitive to it, jettison your planned argument, and redraft your document with the new, fully developed argument in place. Often this new draft will give you even more ideas, or—and this sometimes happens—confirm that your original plan was correct after all. For this reason, don't overwrite your drafts, but save them as entirely separate documents: memo draft 1; memo draft 2; and so on. The most efficient way to label these documents is to use a unique name and the date of draft: "Legal Writing first memo October 4 draft;" "Legal Writing first memo October 10 draft;" and so on.

There's no correct number of drafts you should write, although it would be surprising if your best work surfaces in the first or second drafts. Just remember that the drafting process continues until the cut-off date you've set for the final draft and that you should be rewriting right up until that point.

Chapter 3

Writing It Down

Now that you've gone through the preparatory work, planned your final and intermediate deadlines, outlined your analysis, thought through your issues, and done some research, it's time to start writing. I said in the introduction that this manual wouldn't teach you how to write like a lawyer. But there are some aspects of the writing process that can be lost while you're learning about legal writing, so it seems useful to set them down here.

Two important cautions are in order if you're in law school. First, if a point you read in this manual seems to contradict a point you've read in your assigned writing textbook, follow the textbook. Second, if your teacher contradicts a point in the manual, follow your teacher's instructions. That's common sense, but it also follows the first rule of good writing: write for your reader. In this case, your reader is the teacher who will read, comment on, and ultimately evaluate your work. It's that teacher's expectations you must satisfy, so if something I say here goes against your teacher's expectations, you won't help yourself by blindly following my advice.

With those cautions in mind, let's take a look at some simple steps you can take to adopt a clean legal writing style. Unfortunately, what's considered today to be good legal writing is not necessarily what's considered to be good writing in other academic disciplines and also differs radically from the way lawyers and judges used to write. That means that as a first year student, the only examples of legal writing you are likely to see—the cases in your various textbooks—are not often very helpful. Put simply, the judges writing these decisions were often bad legal writers, based on what we think of today as good legal writing. And if you're working in a law firm, you'll probably be exposed to some good writing—and a lot of bad writing.

Ultimately, in order to develop proficiency as a legal writer, you'll not only have to change some of your present writing habits; you'll also have to avoid following the example of much of the legal writing you are required to read.

A. Use Plain English

Using plain English may well be frustrating to lawyers who have acquired a lot of impressive words in their time. Surely the field of law, more than any other, is the one where these gloriously long, or obscure, or (more accurately) long *and* obscure words belong.

It used to be true that lawyers delighted in using words that weren't part of most people's vocabulary, and there are still many lawyers out there who enjoy tossing around words that send readers scurrying to their dictionaries whenever they encounter them. But for a contemporary practitioner, this is not a desirable result. If judges are the intended audience and they must stop reading a document in order to look up words to determine their meaning, they will likely resent having to interrupt their reading in order to have their apparent shortcomings in language exposed, even to themselves. And judges don't tend to be sympathetic to the person who forced them to realize they didn't know something.

Moreover, many (if not most) lawyers use obscure words to cover up a gap in analysis. It's the legal equivalent of the magician's blue smoke and mirrors. Whenever you see a lot of long and obscure words in a brief, look closely to see if you can find the gap the opposing lawyer is trying to hide. Usually, you will.

Most writers have a model reader in mind when they write—someone they want to understand and appreciate their work. Ideally, for legal writers, that person should be an intelligent nonlawyer with a good, but not vast, vocabulary. If you can write a brief that person can follow and understand, you've written a brief that a judge will be able to follow without difficulty. If you write for this ideal reader, you'll find that writing clear, understandable legal documents will be much easier.

B. Avoid Foreign Terms

One of the principal effects of this new tendency to use plain English is the removal of foreign phrases from our legal vocabulary. Terms like "collateral estoppel" and "res judicata" are being replaced by terms like "issue preclusion" and "claim preclusion," respectively. The reason is clear: even without having studied Civil Procedure, you would know that "issue preclusion" has something to do with whether someone can assert an issue or whether that person will be prevented from asserting the issue. If you were asked what "collateral estoppel" meant, you'd likely have to look the term up in a legal dictionary. And the definition you'd find would likely speak of issue preclusion.

This isn't to say that you will never use a Latin, French, or other foreign language phrase in your writing. Terms like "prima facie," "habeas corpus," "bona fide," and, of course, "versus" have worked their way so strongly into our legal language and culture that it would be almost impossible to root them out. As a result, it's impossible to issue a blanket ban on legal Latin or French. You should use your discretion as to when to use one of these non-English phrases or words, though you should avoid doing so when there's an acceptable English alternative.

Sometimes you have to use a foreign word or phrase. If the context of your writing compels you to use, for example, the words *Schadenfreude* or *Weltschmertz*, you should set the foreign term apart from the rest of your writing by italicizing or underlining it. Foreign terms that have become part of accepted English—"versus," for example—should not be highlighted. When a term has become part of the English language, it will be listed in any most recent, reliable English dictionary. So when you are in doubt, consult the latest edition of *Webster's Collegiate*, for example.

C. Write in Short Coherent Sentences and Short Coherent Paragraphs

From anyone who reviews your writing, you'll likely hear over and over again that you should write in short sentences. Short sentences require you to compress your thoughts. If you construct each sentence properly, it will contain one idea that connects logically with the sentence immediately preceding it and the one immediately following it. Thus, you will construct a coherent chain of thought that runs through your paragraph, leading the reader gently but firmly through your analysis.

The same principle applies to paragraphs. The paragraph is the engine of your document, the fundamental organizational device of your analysis. Each paragraph should contain only one concept that's fully worked through. Just as with sentences, if you can keep your paragraphs short, coherent, and well focused, they'll help your reader comprehend your analysis with no trouble. And easing your reader through the analysis is one of the important tools a good legal writer uses to reach the ultimate goal of persuading the reader that the writer's position is the correct one.

Fine in theory, but what does the suggestion "Write in short coherent sentences and short coherent paragraphs" mean in practice? On average, try to keep your sentences between 20 and 25 words and your paragraphs between 100 and 150 words, preferably the lower number in each case. Does this mean that each sentence should have 20 words and each paragraph 100 words? Of course not. The key word here is "average." Sometimes your sentences will have fewer than 20 words; sometimes they will have many more.

The point is not only should your writing be coherent (that is, have "flow") but also your sentences should contain only as many words as are necessary to get one point across.

D. Vary Sentence and Paragraph Length and Structure

In fact, you should make sure that your sentences are not all the same length and do not all have the same structure. Nothing gets a reader more bored with your writing than reading pages of sentences each of the same length and each constructed in the same way. Since it's easy to let your writing lapse into a hypnotic rhythm, you need to be careful to vary sentence length and structure. Otherwise, the hypnotized reader will probably not assimilate much of what you have written.

One simple way to spot the "hypnotic" writing rhythm is to look at the way you begin your paragraphs. When writing about cases, for example, it's very easy to get into the habit of beginning successive paragraphs: "In *Smith,...*," "In *Jones,...*," "In *Doe,...*," and so on. Such consecutive paragraph beginnings are not only examples of the "hypnotic" style you should avoid; they also do not constitute good analysis. (It's not the case in which the holding appears that's important; it's the holding itself, so that's what you should lead with.)

Besides editing for consecutive paragraph beginnings, you should also look for potential paragraph divisions you've missed during the drafting phase. As you write, it's likely you'll draft one paragraph that has two or more ideas in it. That's fine. It's important not to be too critical of your writing while you write. But when you edit your work, you should be aware of the necessity of dividing your long paragraphs into separate paragraphs, each containing only one thought or part of the analysis.

The suggested maximum paragraph length of 100-150 words is a way to promote this process. As you're going through your work, look at the length of your paragraphs and, if they go beyond 150 words, look for ways to split them into separate paragraphs. As you become more familiar with this process, a quick scan of a page will tell you if your paragraphs are too long without your having to count the words. Even as a beginning legal writer, though, you should be able to tell that a paragraph spanning a page or more is too long.

E. Organize Your Analysis Using Subheadings

Using subheadings is the most efficient way to tell your reader where you're going. And a reader who knows where you're going is much more likely to follow you than a reader who is trying to figure out where your analysis is leading. In memo writing, your headings can be neutral in tone, serving merely as signposts along the way of your analysis. In writing briefs, however, your subheadings should always be argumentative, and when assembled, they should constitute an outline of your argument.

F. Avoid Footnotes

Footnotes are the darling of academic writing, and you were likely taught as undergraduates that an analysis without footnotes isn't worth reading. Law schools are no exception: your textbooks are probably full of footnotes, and any self-respecting law review article probably has the time-honored ratio of one third text and two thirds footnotes for each page.

But thinking that using footnotes should guide the way you write legal documents is to compare apples and oranges. Textbooks, law review articles—even this manual—are not legal documents like memoranda or briefs: they have different goals and are written in entirely different ways, and it's a mistake to think that the techniques applicable to one group of legal documents should apply to all legal documents.

Many judges will not read footnotes, and busy lawyers and clients will likely have little time for them, either. The reason for this is obvious, and it is something you've experienced yourself. The footnote forces you to move your focus from the text down to the bottom of the page, where you're required to assimilate information that, by its very placement, isn't considered by the writer important enough to be in the main text. The writer then forces the reader's eyes back up the page to continue the analysis.[1]

The worst thing about footnotes is that they're hard to ignore. Even though you know you're not likely to learn much of value from them, the fact there's a footnote indicated means you'll miss something if you don't look at it, and you don't want to miss anything. So you'll probably look down, read the footnote, and come back to the text more irritated than you were before. If you force your reader to yo-yo up and down the page too often, you'll lose a lot of your reader's goodwill, which has been too hard-won to squander on something so unnecessary as footnotes.

So if you have footnotes, look at them honestly. If there's something you really want your reader to read, find a way to incorporate it into the main body of the text. If it's not important enough to be in the main text, maybe it doesn't need to be in the document at all. In that case, cut it. Your reader will thank you and you'll save yourself some space as well.

G. Eliminate Unnecessary Words

It is easier said than done, you might argue, to eliminate unnecessary words from your writing. And, you might ask, what is an unnecessary word anyway? It's a word that can be eliminated from

---

1. Like this. Irritating, isn't it?

your document without doing violence either to the rules of grammar or your argument. Put shortly, it's a word that doesn't carry its weight in a sentence.

There are many ways to eliminate unnecessary words. Learning these techniques, and applying them ruthlessly, will help you now and in the future, when you're faced with the task of editing a lengthy brief down to meet a tight page- or word-limit.

i. Avoid the Passive Voice

We often hear the advice to avoid using the passive-voice verb but often we ignore it, either because we forget the advice or because we don't want to worry about grammar when we're trying to write a complicated memorandum or brief. But it's good advice because it helps us save some words and thus makes our writing better.

Before you avoid the passive voice, however, you have to know what it is. Put simply, if the subject of the sentence acts upon a part of speech later in the sentence, the subject is considered the "actor" and the verb is in the active voice—"The cat *sat* on the mat"—but if the subject is acted upon by a part of speech later in the sentence, that part of speech is considered the "actor" and the verb is in the passive voice—"The mat *was sat* upon by the cat." Another way to spot the passive voice is to look for the combination of a "be" verb (is, are, was, were, been, being, am) with a past participle. Any combination of a "be" verb and a word ending in "ed" (or an equivalent—"en," for example, as in "bitten") will result in the passive voice. For example, "is estopped," "were granted," "been determined," "was discovered," "are referenced," "be declared," "was given," and "being sued" are all passive-verb constructions.

Another way to spot the passive voice is to see if you can add an actor to the end of a sentence. If the sentence makes sense after the addition, the verb is likely in the passive voice. So, for example, if you add the actor "Jane" to the end of the sentence "Jane built the house," the result, "Jane built the house by Jane," makes no sense, and the original verb is therefore in the active voice. By contrast, if you add the actor "Jane" to the end of the sentence "The house was built," the result, "The house was built by Jane," makes perfect sense, and the verb is therefore in the passive voice.[2]

It doesn't matter what technique you use to spot the passive voice, but it's important that you learn to spot it and avoid it when you find it. Unfortunately for us, legal writing thrives on the use of the passive voice. Lawyers and judges like the passive voice's emphasis on the subject of the sentence rather than on the parts of the sentence after the verb, so passive constructions, like those listed above, are common in legal writing.

One possible reason for the law's overuse of the passive voice is the opportunity it offers to obscure the actor. The passive voice allows lawyers to say "the action was taken" without saying who took the action, and sometimes lawyers can use this kind of obfuscation to their advantage. A defense lawyer, for example, might want to concede that someone committed a crime but not that the lawyer's client committed it. Saying "a crime was committed" allows the lawyer to make that concession without identifying the actor.

So there are times when the passive voice has strategic value. But these occasions occur less frequently than you may think, so you should always be able to justify your use of the passive voice by pointing to a specific advantage to be gained from it. If you can't, eliminate it. You'll save space, since the active voice almost always uses fewer words than the passive. (For example, "The cat sat on the mat" contains six words but "The mat was sat upon by the cat" contains eight words.) Also, your writing will be tighter and more readable.

ii. Avoid "Be" Verbs

Not only do "be" verbs help promote the passive voice, they lead to wordiness generally, so you should avoid them where possible.

---

2. My thanks to Jarrett Perlow for this suggestion.

Some have advocated an almost total rejection of "be" verbs in their writing.[3] Even if you do not go to this extreme, if you can reduce your use of "is," "are," "was," "were," "been," "being," "be," and "am," your writing would improve.

iii. Avoid "-tion" Words

Try not to use words ending in "-tion," either. This suggestion may be difficult. Lawyers love to use verbs that have been altered to act as nouns, so you'll see plenty of examples of such words in the reading you do for other classes. And you probably came to law school with a burning desire to use phrases like "take into consideration" or "in mitigation of." But the payoff's worth the effort of avoiding such phrases. Leave "-tion" words out of your writing, and it will be free from excess verbiage and therefore cleaner and easier to read.

The "-tion" ending is one of the signs that a verb has been forced to live as a noun: in the jargon of grammarians, the verb has been "nominalized." When this happens, one word like the verb "mitigate" becomes the "nominalized," three-word phrase "in mitigation of." Also, "examine" becomes "conduct an examination of"; "describe" becomes "provide a description of"; and so on. Other endings besides "-tion" can show this "nominalization" as well. So beware of any word ending in "-al," "-ment," "-ant," "-ence," "-ent," "-ancy," "-ency," "-ance," and "-ity." Although not every word with one of these endings has been nominalized, many words have been, so it's easier to eliminate them altogether from your vocabulary than it is to go back and figure out whether each word ending in "-tion" (and so on) is acceptable.

---

3. For a description of this highly disciplined style of writing, see Christopher Wren's article *E-Prime, Briefly: A Lawyer's Experiment With Writing In E-Prime*, published in 2002 in volume 48 of *Clarity*.

iv. Eliminate Adverbs

Adverbs, like all parts of speech, have an important place in English grammar. But they have no place in legal writing. They convey little or no meaning, and they promote lazy use of the language. ("Why find a more exact and precise verb when you can modify your current verb with an adverb?" the lazy writer may ask.) In addition, adverbs clutter up written English.

Adverbs modify verbs, adjectives, and other adverbs. An "-ly" placed at the end of a word often—though not always—indicates an adverb. One simple test for overusing adverbs is to set the "search" function in your word processing program to find every word ending in "-ly." Then, if one of the words turns out to be an adverb (*sickly*, for example, is an adjective, though it ends in "-ly"), see if you need the adverb or if you can find a more precise verb that would allow you to delete it. For example, I could have written, "See if you *really* need the adverb...." Using *really* would have been correct, and the adverb wouldn't have disrupted the meaning or flow of the sentence. But I didn't need it since it didn't add anything to the meaning of the sentence. In fact, it would have cluttered the sentence. So omitting it saved me a word.

H. Avoid Legalisms

Nothing makes us sound more like people trying to sound like lawyers than using flowery language that obscures, rather than reveals, the writer's meaning. Whether most legal terms ever had any other purpose than to obscure meaning is open to debate. There's no question, though, that lawyerisms (or "legalisms") are death to clear writing, and because clear writing is what you want to produce, you should never allow a legalism into the final draft of anything you write.

Legalisms are words or phrases like "pursuant to," "inasmuch as," "brought an action against," "said" (used as an adjective—as in "said action"), "same" (used as a pronoun—as in "equivalent to same"), and "the case at bar." Their plain English equivalents are simpler and clearer: "pursuant to" becomes "under" or "by"; "inasmuch as" becomes "because"; "brought an action against" becomes "sued"; "said" becomes, depending on the context, "the," "this," or "that"; "same" becomes "it" or "them"; and "the case at bar" becomes "here" or, simply, "this case."

You'll lose no credibility when you omit these legalisms from your writing. In fact, no one will even notice they're not there. What you'll gain is a clearer, more intelligible sentence each time one of these words or phrases is dropped and a simple word or two is put in its place.

I. Avoid Other Wordy Phrases

Even when they're not using legalisms, lawyers are often wordy writers. And wordy writing is never good writing. Here are a few more expressions that often crop up in legal writing, together with their simpler alternatives. "At the present time" should be "now"; "because of the fact that" should be "because"; "excessive number of" should be "too many"; "in the near future" should be "soon"; "notwithstanding the fact that" should be "although"; "on a daily basis" should be "daily"; "take into consideration" (a "-tion" word) should be "consider"; and "the majority of" should be "most."

Replacing these wordy phrases with their simpler counterparts doesn't change the meaning of what you're writing. The only difference between, for example, "because of the fact that" and "because" is that the wordy version uses five words and the simple version uses one. Also, "because" is clearer.

So simplify your words and phrases: you may not sound like someone who has a big vocabulary but you'll almost certainly sound like you know what you're saying. More importantly, your reader will also know what you're saying. And isn't the easy transfer of knowledge between writer and reader the core of what we're trying to accomplish as legal writers?

J. Keep the Subject, Verb, and Object Close Together

No book about writing style can fail to introduce a few grammatical concepts. But don't worry if you can't now identify a subject or an object in a sentence, or even if you can't find a verb. Suggesting that you should keep the subject, verb, and object close together in a sentence is just a technical way of suggesting what you normally do in speaking outside the context of the legal profession. When you think you must write like a lawyer in order to impress people, the word order of your sentences fractures and you stop making sense. To fix these grammatical "fractures," all you need to do is rewrite the sentence so that you sound like one nonlawyer speaking "naturally" to another.

Here's a sentence as if it were naturally spoken: "The defendant filed a motion to dismiss." In the sentence, "defendant" is the subject, "filed" is the verb, and "motion to dismiss" is the object. Simple, straightforward, easy to understand.

Here's the damage many lawyers would do to that straightforward sentence: "The defendant, by and through its attorney Polly Peachum of the law firm McHeath, Peachum, and Lockitt, LLP, and for purposes of seeking a speedy resolution of the baseless claims brought against it by plaintiff, Jane Suer, filed, in the Circuit Court for Fictitious County, on August 1, 2002, and pursuant to Rule 12(b)(6) of the State of Litigation Rules of Civil Procedure, a motion to dismiss."

What happened in this "fractured" sentence? Exactly who did exactly what? And exactly what was done and why? Would you naturally speak in such a broken and pretentious way? And this sentence is a simple one compared to some you'll have to read as a lawyer.

Why is this sentence such a mess compared to the first one? Because in the first sentence there are no words between the subject and the verb, and there is only one word—"a"—between the verb and the object. But in the second sentence there are 35 words between the subject and the verb, and there are 26 words between the verb and the object. (Each part of the date counts as a word, and "12(b)(6)" counts as a word—because there are no spaces between the subparts.).

Certainly the second sentence has more information in it, but it's information obtained at a cost: if you're like most readers, you can't understand the sentence containing it. In order to comprehend its meaning, you likely had to read the sentence at least twice, and probably three or four times. Imagine what it's like to read 50 pages of sentences like that. More to the point, imagine how a judge would react if faced with reading 50 pages of your sentences written like that.

So if you should happen to write an overlong, poorly constructed sentence that will confuse the reader, how should you revise it? The answer's simple. Follow the rule about sentence length by making three or four short sentences out of one long one. In each of these sentences, keep the subject, verb, and object close together; write in the active voice; don't use legal jargon; and be sensitive to your reader's patience. In London, at certain Underground stops, a computerized voice synthetically enjoins you, "Mind the gap"—to warn you there's a gap between the door and the platform. Tape that injunction to your computer's monitor, and every time you're editing your writing, make sure you "mind the gap" between your sentence's subject, verb, and object.

K. Use Past Tense When Discussing Cases

This rule should be simple to follow, but for some reason it causes trouble for many law students and lawyers. If you think about the sense of what you're writing, however, it should be easy to correct errors in tense.

Let's consider some judicial language: "The crucial question, therefore, in many Eleventh Amendment cases is whether an agency or official is properly characterized as an arm of the state, or of the local government." The quotation is from a Fourth Circuit case, *Harter v. Vernon*, 101 F.3d 334, 337 (4th Cir. 1996). For present purposes, don't worry about any substantive significance the quote might have.

If, in my analysis of this issue, I was to write "In *Harter*, the Fourth Circuit concludes that the proper characterization of the individual's relationship with the State is the crucial 11th Amendment question," I would have made an accurate summary of the holding, and, taken out of context, the sentence is grammatically correct. But taken *in* context, the sentence isn't accurate because the Fourth Circuit isn't presently concluding anything at all in *Harter*. It did some concluding in 1996, but the court's action was over when it issued its opinion on November 22, 1996. So if I was to write, "The Fourth Circuit *concludes....*," I would be wrong. To be correct, I should have written, "The Fourth Circuit *concluded....*"

Some of you may disagree, maintaining that the court's action in *Harter*—or in any other case—is frozen in time, frozen in a sort of permanent legal present outside of normal time, and that since present tense is to be preferred over all others (everything else being equal), it's perfectly correct to use the present tense in referring to court action in cases. But while the words in the case don't change so that it may be technically correct to write, "In *Harter*, the Fourth Circuit *concludes....*," it's more correct to consider the court's *current* state regarding the case—i.e., the court has already acted upon it—as opposed to the present tense language of the case itself, and therefore to write about such cases in the past tense.

There are two other reasons for using the past tense to discuss cases, both of them as compelling as my previous reason. First, it's just simpler to do so. You have only one rule to remember: since the case was decided in the past, *always* use the past tense. Otherwise, you'll have to constantly make sure you're using the correct tense and constantly make sure that each part of speech in your paragraph agrees with whatever tense you have chosen.

Second, sticking to the past tense will make your writing easier to read. If you write about some cases in the past tense and some in the present, your reader will be bounced around through time, never quite sure when you're going next. If you stick to the past, your reader will feel comfortable, secure, and trusting—exactly what you want your reader to feel.

There's yet another reason for you to write case analysis in the past tense, a reason not nearly as valid as the previous ones, even though it might be the most important reason of all: simply put, lawyers have traditionally written about cases in the past tense.

L. Watch for Agreement between Nouns and Pronouns

This rule can be tricky. Nearly everyone knows that singular nouns take singular pronouns and plural nouns take plural pronouns: for example, a male lawyer is referred to as "he," "his," or "him," depending on the function of the pronoun in the sentence; in the same way, several female lawyers are referred to as "they," "their," "theirs," or "them."

A problem arises in distinguishing singular nouns from plural nouns, and, for lawyers, it's an especially tricky problem for two reasons. First, some of the singular entities we deal with have a distressing tendency to look like plural ones and can fool us into making wrong choices in agreement. Second, in our well-intentioned, and correct, desire to stay away from sexist language, we often turn to the plural "they" instead of the awkward-sounding singular (e.g., "he or she"; "his or her"; etc.). Examples should help to clarify both of these problems.

i. Singular Entities

In legal writing, the two most confusing singular entities are "court" and "corporation." The reason for the confusion is understandable. There are nine justices on the United States Supreme Court; there are usually at least three judges on a federal appellate panel; and even though there's only one trial judge, most trial "courts" have multiple judges. But when the Supreme Court issues an opinion, it speaks as the "Court"—as a singular, monolithic entity, not as a collection of nine justices—so it must be referred to in the singular. If you are still confused, think of "court" as a collective noun referring to a group (like a "gaggle" of geese, a "flock" of birds, a "murder" of crows, a "parliament" of owls, a "court" of judges, and so on). Collective nouns, even though they describe multiple components, are nearly always singular in legal contexts.

Appellate courts don't always help us make the correct choice in agreement. In their opinions, judges (and justices) often write that, as a Court, "we" held something in a previous opinion. The Supreme Court does this all the time. Here's an example from a recent case: "In these cases, we decide whether the District Court properly enjoined a Mississippi state court's proposed congressional redistricting plan and whether it properly fashioned its own congressional reapportionment plan rather than order at-large elections." *Branch v. Smith*, 538 U.S. 254, 258 (2003).

Unfortunately for the novice legal writer, the Court can make the choice it wants in noun-pronoun agreement, but the rest of us are bound by the rules of grammar. So regardless of how a court may refer to itself, the best practical advice for the rest of us is to think of every court as a singular, not a plural, entity.

Therefore, you should never use the word "they" to refer to "the court." The word "court" is singular and neuter, and therefore the pronoun "it" should be used in reference to it. The same is true for a corporation, company, or other corporate entity. So you should write not, "When Widget Company made its Neuewidget, *they* made a flawed product," but, "When Widget Company made its Neuewidget, *it* made a flawed product." Using a plural pronoun to refer to a court or a corporate entity is one of the most common writing mistakes made by practicing lawyers, and it's easily fixed by careful proofreading.

ii. Sexist Language

Avoiding sexist language is tricky when we also want to make our nouns and pronouns agree with each other. We write "they" instead of the awkward "he or she" or "him or her" because we want to avoid characterizing a person with a gender if we don't know whether the person is male or female. For years, writers used the masculine gender pronoun in places where a non-gender-specific pronoun would be more appropriate—a practice no longer acceptable. But using "they" as an alternative in referring to a singular noun doesn't work because such usage violates a fundamental grammatical principle: a singular noun always takes a singular pronoun. And there will always be a reader out there who will call you on any noun-pronoun agreement mistakes you make.

M. Avoiding Sexist Language

But the instinct to avoid sexist language is a good one. In the twenty-first century, there's no excuse for using language to reinforce sexual stereotypes that have no foundation in reality.

If you haven't been persuaded that using sexist language is wrong, consider this: sexist language is imprecise and can lead to confusion—which you, as a lawyer, should try to avoid at all costs. If you use the male pronoun, are you writing specifically about one or more males? Or are you using a male pronoun generically—that is, to refer to a female as well as a male? The context might give the reader some clues, but not always.

If you're still unconvinced, think about the practical result of using sexist language. You may believe that it's appropriate to refer to a judge as "he" in a brief because, in your world, all judges are, or should be, male. But if your brief is read by a female judge, you won't likely be as persuasive as you would if you'd selected a gender-neutral way of referring to the judge.

Of course, the easiest way to avoid sexist language is to avoid thinking in a sexist way. That should solve about 90 percent of the problem. To solve the remaining 10 percent, there are several techniques you can use:

- Don't use expressions that carry sexist assumptions. There are many of these around—for example, "a member of the fairer (gentler) sex," "a manly effort," "mankind"—and avoiding them will not reduce your power of language.

- Use expressions that are gender-neutral when possible ("worker" instead of "workman," "reasonable person" instead of "reasonable man," "chair" instead of "chairman," "representative" instead of "spokesman," and so on).

- Use plural constructions: "Attorneys have ethical obligations to their clients," not, "A lawyer has an ethical obligation to his client." The problem in noun-pronoun agreement discussed earlier stems from a half-hearted and incorrect implementation of this practice.

- Don't use masculine pronouns unless you're referring to a specific male person. The simplest solution here is to eliminate all personal pronouns from the sentence: "A lawyer owes a client an ethical obligation," instead of, "A lawyer owes his client an ethical obligation."

- Repeat the noun instead of using a pronoun: "A lawyer's actions should reflect the ethical obligation the lawyer owes to a client," instead of, "A lawyer's actions should reflect the ethical obligation he owes to his client."

One technique you should avoid is the alternating use of "he" and "she" — that is, using masculine pronouns in one paragraph and feminine pronouns in the next, masculine in the next, and so on. Such usage can sometimes lead to interesting results — giving a judge a sex-change in the middle of a case analysis, for example. And it's almost impossible to stick to the alternating pattern rigidly. Moreover, this technique reduces your ability to make a specific reference to one gender or the other when required, and any technique that limits your ability to articulate your analysis clearly should be avoided.

You might ask if avoiding sexist language, although perhaps a good idea, won't turn your writing into a stilted, politically correct, but sterile piece of work. The answer is no. With its informal and mostly conversational style, this manual is hardly "stilted" and "sterile," and yet it was written without any gender-specific language (expect for the examples of sexist language to avoid). Avoiding gender-specific language will not necessarily make *your* writing "stilted" and "sterile," either.

N. Avoid Throat Clearing

We all know the feeling of being about to say something but being unable to get the sentence going. So we say "eh" or "um" or "like." These "throat-noises" don't mean anything in any context, and they're not meant to convey meaning. They're just a way of getting your brain and body conditioned for the sentence that's still waiting to emerge. (Note that the word "like," in its colloquial, throat-clearing usage, should be dropped from every lawyer's vocabulary because of its potential for abuse and the hostile reaction from judges and other lawyers such abuse usually arouses).

These throat-clearing noises aren't a good strategy in spoken English. They become verbal tics that can irritate a listener very quickly. But we all have them and most of us are willing to forgive them in others. In writing, though, there's no excuse for throat clearing, and you should hunt down and remove any instances of it.

What does written throat clearing "look like"? The answer is, "any words at the beginning of a sentence that don't carry meaning." Here are some examples: "the point is"; "it is clear that"; "a review of the record will demonstrate that"; "by means of"; "it is significant that"; "it is more likely than not that"; "the question of whether"; "there is no doubt that"; "notwithstanding the fact that."

Phrases like these are just a waste of space. They prepare your reader for a point at some indeterminate future time, but they don't give your reader the point you're about to make. They also make your writing flabby and bloated. For these reasons, you should omit them.

Be careful, however, because some sentence and paragraph beginnings may look like throat clearing but aren't. These are words or phrases that link the present sentence to the previous sentence or paragraph. Writing textbooks and writing teachers speak about the value of these links (also called "transitions") in much greater detail. For the moment, however, you should recognize that words like "and," "but," "moreover," "also," and "however," and phrases like "in contrast," "in addition," and "what is more" are useful links, or bridges, between portions of your argument. Because they serve a role in making your meaning clear, these aren't throat-clearing words or phrases. Indeed (another linking word), your writing will be more coherent if you use linking words and phrases carefully to make your analysis as seamless as possible.

Legal writing presents a particular opportunity for writers to clear their throats. You may have been told, or will be told, that paragraphs should open with topic sentences and that rule statements derived from legal authority are particularly useful ones. As a result, lawyers and law students will often start a paragraph with a sentence such as "In *Illinois v. Rodriguez*, the Supreme Court noted that the only reason police officers seek third-party consent before searching property is to avoid the inconvenience of getting a warrant. 497 U.S. 177, 190 (1990)."

The sentence is redundant because the first 9 of its 29 words—almost a third of the sentence—constitute unnecessary throat clearing. That this rule comes from *Illinois v. Rodriguez* becomes obvious if the name of the case is removed from the sentence and is placed where it belongs—in the accompanying citation. From the citation, the reader will learn that the Supreme Court decided the case.

With pruning, and transfer of language, the sentence now becomes: "The only reason police officers seek third-party consent before searching property is to avoid the inconvenience of getting a warrant. *Illinois v. Rodriguez,* 497 U.S. 177, 190 (1990)." The rule statement is now an effective one, as well as a clear and direct topic sentence for a paragraph. The information about the law is given in the sentence, and the information in the citation can be considered or ignored and does not impede the flow of the analysis. And at 20 words, the textual sentence is almost a third shorter than the original.

O. Avoid Split Infinitives

An infinitive consists of the word "to" followed by a verb. A *split* infinitive occurs when a writer places an adverb between the two words. Perhaps the most famous split infinitive is *Star Trek*'s "to boldly go," with "to go" the infinitive and "boldly" the adverb that elbows its way between the infinitive's two parts. Split infinitives are controversial. Most grammarians know that the prejudice against split infinitives has no basis in English grammar and is therefore irrational. But many nongrammarians—including many judges and senior attorneys—believe that splitting an infinitive is always a mistake and therefore signifies an illiterate lawyer.

And that's the reason I suggest you avoid splitting infinitives. Grammarians know that a split infinitive is socially (and grammatically) acceptable, but many—even most—readers of legal documents aren't grammarians. They believe, wrongly, that the split infinitive is a fundamental grammatical error. So if they see a split infinitive in your work, such readers will believe you've made a mistake, and this "mistake" is one you cannot defend yourself against since you'll never know you made the "mistake" in the first place. The reader will simply form a lower opinion of you as a legal writer and move on. Obviously, such an opinion won't advance your writing reputation. Yet it isn't difficult to avoid this self-inflicted "wound": at worst, you'll have to move the words in a sentence around a little. So if you see a phrase that looks like something Captain Kirk would say, change it. Safety first is the policy in legal writing.

P. Ending Sentences with Prepositions

In school you may have been advised never to end a sentence with a preposition. This advice is simply wrong. For as long as there's been standardized grammar, grammarians have agreed that there's nothing wrong with ending a sentence with a preposition.

That's the good news. The bad news is that I advise you as a legal writer to avoid ending your sentences with prepositions. First, unless handled with care, sentences ending in prepositions sound inelegant. (In the sentence "What are you afraid of?" the "of" juts out from the back of the sentence like a sharp object.) Second, the readers of your legal document were probably taught the same, technically incorrect information about sentence endings as you (and they haven't had access to this manual to learn their mistake!). So don't let your readers' ignorance harm you. The safe course is to keep prepositions within the main body of the sentence.

Q. Beginning Sentences with Conjunctions

But we can take a reader's prejudice too far. Although you may have learned not to begin sentences with conjunctions, feel free to do exactly that. There's no rule against beginning a sentence with a conjunction, and conjunctions—because of their strong connective power—forge good links between sentences and paragraphs, and even between sections. These links are a crucial technique in writing coherent prose—which keeps the reader moving down the page and wanting to turn the page to see what comes next. To begin sentences with conjunctions won't turn your brief into a literary masterpiece, but it's not wrong to do so.

Chapter 4

Punctuation

Most students come to law school with a general understanding of the rules of punctuation. Unfortunately, this isn't enough to get by. You don't need to be a grammar expert to survive as a legal writer, but you do need to have a solid grasp of punctuation rules to meet the expectations of most legal readers.

A skimming of this section may confirm what you already know about punctuation, or it may give you an insight into some of the things you need to learn. So here's a synopsis of the most important rules of punctuation. The good news is that there are only fourteen punctuation marks you need to be concerned with, and some of them have only one use. The bad news is that correct punctuation is one of the hallmarks of a careful writer, and almost every legal reader who counts will know all these fourteen well.

A. The Apostrophe

The apostrophe is the least understood and most misused of all punctuation marks. Its misuse can drive many readers into a towering fury. And for many legal readers—including judges and those attorneys who read writing samples from potential employees—the correct use of the apostrophe is one of the indicators of a legal writer's competence.

The reason for all this attention is simple: since the apostrophe is a flexible mark, its usage can vary in several different ways. When the legal writer confuses its varied usage and places an apostrophe where it doesn't belong, or omits it from a word that needs it, a sentence originally correct can become hopelessly incomprehensible. But once you understand the apostrophe's various uses, it's not that difficult to use it correctly.

i. Omission

We use apostrophes to indicate the omission of letters in a word. The result is called a contraction—usually colloquial in usage. Therefore, it's one you won't use much as a legal writer. As an example, look at the preceding sentence and the word "it's." This is a contracted form of the words "it is," with the space between the two words and the letter "i" of "is" omitted. The apostrophe is our way of showing this omission. A contraction without its apostrophe is written as wrongly as if it has been misspelled.

Note that in the last sentence of the previous paragraph, the word "its" has no apostrophe. That's because the word, used in its possessive-case context, doesn't require one. If, on the other hand, I'd written "It's important to note that....," an apostrophe would have been necessary. One of the most prevalent ways of misusing the apostrophe is to insert one before the letter "s" in every word ending in "s." Just remember: before you set down anything on a page, you should first know its meaning and usage in context before you include it. This caution counts for punctuation marks just as much as it does for words. So whenever you see an apostrophe in your writing, ask yourself why it's there and if it's correct in context.

ii. Possession

The apostrophe's second principal use is to indicate possession or, more accurately, the possessive case. For example, in the previous sentence, no letter is missing between the "e" and the "s" in the word "apostrophe's," and yet the apostrophe is necessary: "The apostrophe's second principal use...." can also be written, "The second principal use of the apostrophe...." The first version is made possible by the apostrophe because it flags the omission of "of the" to indicate possession. This use of the apostrophe isn't a colloquial one and will appear in your legal writing all the time.

Other examples of this usage of the apostrophe are "Joan's book" (the book Joan owns or possesses); "the court's ruling" (the ruling of the court); and "Jones's lawsuit." This last example is controversial. Many of you have learned that when a personal name ends in "s" and is used in the possessive case, the apostrophe should follow the "s" but should not itself be followed by another "s". According to this rule, the last example would read, "Jones' lawsuit." But with the exception of some names of more than one syllable—like "Sophocles" (which would "sound" quite awkward with the additional "s," as in "Sophocles's"), most writers on contemporary usage agree that it is preferable to include the additional "s."

This contemporary preference can be tricky: some of your readers may not be familiar it, and you can't drop a footnote to explain your decision to include the additional "s." Of course, a safe way to avoid the problem is simply to omit the letter. Any reader who knows enough about grammar to question your decision will also know of the two ways of using the apostrophe to indicate the possessive case of personal names. But adding the "s" to the apostrophe is now correct contemporary American usage and omitting it is wrong.

To indicate the possessive case of most *plural* nouns ending in "s," you need to add only an apostrophe. For example, "the case of the defendants" and "the motion of the plaintiffs" can be written "the defendants' case" and "the plaintiffs' motion," respectively.

iii. Misusing Apostrophes

Apostrophes should never be used in two situations. First, they should never be placed before the final "s" in a plural noun ending in "s." Obviously, you would never (I hope!) form the plural of "attorney" by writing "attorney's." Second, apostrophes are never used to form the plurals of letters or numerals. A few decades ago it was acceptable to write, "In the 1970's, the feminist movement began to gain political influence." In contemporary usage, however, "1970s" is the correct plural form—without the apostrophe. Similarly, today we write "ABCs" to indicate the plural, not "ABC's."

B. Brackets

There are many kinds of brackets. The computer you're probably using recognizes four types, each having its own set of rules: (1) parentheses, ( )—the most common type; (2) square brackets, [ ]; (3) what we might term "ornate brackets," { }; and (4) angled brackets, < >. Angled brackets have come into their own in these days of the Internet, where they're used to mark the beginnings and ends of URLs—for example, <http://www.peachum.com>. (This specialized use, though, is the only one you will likely encounter in legal writing.) You will often use parentheses (as you would in any kind of writing). The "ornate bracket" you will never use in legal writing. The most common type of bracket found in legal documents is the square bracket, so when we speak of brackets below, we'll be referring to the square ones.

In legal writing, brackets are almost always employed within quotations. You should use them when you want to add something to a quoted passage, such as an explanation, a commentary, or punctuation marks, or when you want to substitute a word or phrase for the original language in the quotation. For example, "Peter Grimes was guilty of child abuse and murder" could become "Peter Grimes[, a local fisherman,] was guilty of child abuse and murder;" and "Rosina Almaviva's divorce petition was granted" could become "[Plaintiff's] divorce petition was granted."

You can also use brackets to change a character within quoted material. You most often do this when you use just part of the original quotation. For example, you may wish to shorten the original "Accordingly, this Court finds that plaintiff's appeal should be denied" by writing, "[P]laintiff's appeal should be denied." Note that the "p" in the original "plaintiff's" has been capitalized, since in the process of shortening the quotation you've placed the word first in your sentence. To indicate that the word was not originally capitalized, you should place brackets around the "P." By a similar process, you can incorporate the original sentence "Defendant's cross-appeal should be granted" into your document by writing, "The appellate court held that '[d]efendant's cross-appeal should be granted.'" (Here, of course, the original "D" is lowercased—"d"—and brackets are placed around it.)

The bracket's final use is to mark the omission of part of a word within a quotation. For example, the original quotation "Defendant assumes that the Court will ignore its actions in this matter" you can incorporate into your document by writing, "The Court was not impressed by Widget Company's defense, noting that it must 'assume[] that the Court will ignore its actions in this matter.'" (Here, of course, the syntax of *your* sentence requires that the original "d" in "assumed" be omitted. To indicate the omission, you use brackets.) Note that you can only use brackets in this way if less than an entire word is missing. If one or more words have been removed, you must use three spaced ellipsis dots (…) to indicate the omission.

C. The Comma

The comma is the second most used punctuation mark after the period (which closes almost every sentence). Writers often sprinkle their sentences with commas, seemingly dropping them in at random, on no rational basis. Perhaps the reason for such randomness is the often forbidding complexity of the rules for comma use. But just the technical difficulty of knowing how to use commas correctly isn't a good enough reason, because commas are best understood as signs that help our writing simulate speech patterns, and if we'd "listen" to our writing, comma use would be much simpler to understand.

So while you'll be given the technical rules here, consider trying the following as well. Read that last sentence aloud. If you read it naturally, your voice probably dropped after the word "here," and then you paused for a second and then continued with "consider." So when you reach a natural pause in the sentence, that's a good sign you may need a comma. You may need other marks, such as parentheses (if you've written a parenthetical clause like this one, for example). Or you may need dashes—which often function like parentheses—instead. But consider the comma as your first alternative. "Listening" to your writing is important for a number of reasons, but placing commas correctly is one of the most important of them.

Now, for the technical rules:

First, you should use a comma to join independent clauses linked by a coordinating conjunction. (Just to remind you, the coordinating conjunctions are "and," "but," "or," "nor," "yet," "for," and "so.") Some examples follow, with each coordinating conjunction underlined that joins the independent clauses: "This is a form and style manual, and it is a very helpful one at that"; "The plaintiff's lawyer was well prepared, but the defendant's lawyer hadn't even looked at the file"; "The facts were in plaintiff's favor, yet the defendant won"; "The defendant's brief was well written, so the judge was familiar with the defendant's position"; and so on. Note that the comma should be placed after the first independent clause and before the conjunction.

The comma is also used to set off transitions at the beginnings of sentences. These can be one word: "Significantly, the plaintiff's lawyer emphasized the facts and stayed away from the law." Or they can be entire phrases: "Looking instead to the law of the case, the court found in favor of the defendant." In addition, commas are used to set off introductory subordinate clauses: "If the plaintiff wants to argue negligence, it should be prepared for the defendant to assert a contributory negligence defense."

Another use of the comma—especially common in legal writing—is to separate items in a list. This usage—also known as "the serial comma"—requires you to place a comma not only after each item but also before the coordinating conjunction which precedes the final item in the list (despite what you may have been taught before coming to law school!) For example, in the sentence "The elements of negligence are duty, breach, causation, and damage," a comma is placed between "causation" and "and"—as well as between the other items. (Journalists can omit that final comma, but legal writers cannot.)

A comma is also used in writing out dates and addresses. Use commas to separate the date from the year and the year from the rest of the sentence. And use commas to separate the parts of an address (the street, city, and state) and the address from the rest of the sentence. (One exception: there's no comma between the state and the zip code.) An example: "This was written on June 26, 2005, at 321 Main Street, Nowhere City, ED 09876, by a solitary gentleman on his ninety-ninth birthday. But if you're writing only the month and the year, there's no comma between them (e.g., "June 2005").

There are other acceptable uses for commas, but you should be cautious about employing them in legal writing. For example, you should use commas to separate written from spoken language, as in the example: "After consideration, the judge said, 'Motion denied.'" Here the use of the comma emphasizes that the judge spoke and the actual words the judge used, rather than the legal significance of what the judge said. Because you should almost always be more concerned with the legal significance of a statement than the words used to make that statement, you won't use the comma in this way very often.

You also use commas to set apart a series of adjectives modifying a noun. For example, in the sentence, "The teacher of legal writing was a vindictive, querulous person," a comma separates the two adjectives, each of which describes the person. But here is a tricky exception: If the sentence reads, "The legal writing teacher was a vindictive, querulous teaching assistant," no comma should separate "querulous" from "teaching" since the phrase "teaching assistant" is considered a single "unit"—specifically, an adjective-noun combination—and the two preceding adjectives each modify the unit. Examples of similar constructions are "a sprightly, insightful Asian male"; "a thoughtful, disciplined medical student"; "a speedy, intelligent basketball guard." One test to determine whether or not you use the comma is to rephrase the series of adjectives and the noun into a sentence with a form of the verb "to be" and the word "and" connecting the adjectives. If the sentence makes sense, then insert the comma; if it doesn't, leave it out. For example, does the sentence "The guard was speedy and intelligent and basketball" make complete sense? Of course not. So you'd leave out the comma between the adjective "intelligent" and the adjective "basketball."

A quick rule about use of commas in the context of quotations: if you insert a quotation in the middle of your own sentence and need a comma after the quotation, you should place the comma inside the closing quotation marks of the quotation even if the original quotation had no comma. For example, in the sentence, "When the court observed, 'There is no factual basis to support plaintiff's claim,' it was mistaken," note the comma *inside* the closing mark of the original quotation.

Perhaps the most common error in comma usage is to place the mark between a subject and a verb. You shouldn't write: "The defendant's lawyer, wrote an excellent brief"; you should write: "The defendant's lawyer wrote an excellent brief." You can tell the first sentence misuses the comma because, when you read the sentence aloud, there is no natural pause between "lawyer" and "wrote." This mistake crops up often in contemporary legal writing. My best advice is to read your work aloud during the editing process, paying attention, with your ear, to the commas you've inserted. The ear can catch many comma errors the eye cannot.

D. The Colon

The colon doesn't have as many uses as the comma, but it's still a handy punctuation mark. Its first, and most important, use is to mark the beginning of a list. You should leave two spaces between the introductory colon and the beginning of the list, as well as between each element of the list. In addition, you should place a semicolon after each element (except, of course, the last, which ends with a period). Here's a example of such a list: "Before a class can be certified, a plaintiff must first prove: (a) that there are so many class members that individual joinder is impracticable; (b) that the class members have common claims; (c) that the class representative's claims are typical of the claims of the other class members; (d) that the class representative is adequate to represent the interests of the class; and (e) that at least one or more of the provisions of Rule 23(b) is met."

Of course, you can also use commas to separate the elements of a list. So how do you know when to use commas and when to use semicolons? If the list is broken into discrete subparts and uses subpart indicators—(a), (b), (c), (1), (2), (3), and so on—you should use semicolons. (Note that I didn't use semicolons in the last sentence to separate the parts of the inserted phrase because I wasn't using the terms as subpart indicators but as the elements of the list itself.) Other than that exception, a general rule is to use semicolons if your list has more than five elements.

You can also use a colon to separate clauses or phrases within a sentence, but only when there's a definite break between them and not before a conjunction. In the preceding sentence, for instance, a colon would not have been appropriate ("You can also use a colon

to separate clauses or phrases within a sentence: but only when....").
That's because while the comma indicates only a breath of a pause,
the colon indicates a hard stop. You use the colon, therefore, when
the second clause or phrase is related to, but distinct from, the first
part of the sentence. For example: "Widget Company is guilty: it
negligently manufactured a defective product that injured the plaintiff." One tip is to think of the colon as shorthand for "because" or
"and here's why." If you substitute those words in place of the colon
and the sentence makes sense, then your use of the colon will probably work.[1]

Another of the colon's uses is to mark the beginning of a block
quote. Right after the last word of your text, before you space down
to begin the block quote, insert a colon to show that what follows
is the quote and not your language.

Finally, you should use a colon after the salutation in a business
letter: "Dear Mr. Grimes:"—for example.

E. Dashes

There are two types of dashes in standard punctuation. They're
usually referred to as "em" dashes and "en" dashes. The "em" dash
takes up the amount of space used by the printed letter "m." The "en"
dash, predictably enough, takes up the space of the printed letter "n."

To avoid any confusion, when I speak of a dash, I mean the mark
produced when you type two hyphens side by side (i.e., —) on your
keyboard.—(The hyphen is the character located between "0" and
"=".) Your word processor may smooth these two characters into
one "em" dash. Allow it to do this.

The only acceptable use of the "em" dash in legal writing is to set
off parenthetical phrases within sentences or at the ends of sentences. There are many examples of the "em" dash in this manual—

---

1. My thanks to Julie McKinstry for this suggestion.

and here's another one. You should not overuse this mark of punctuation. I've used it a lot in this manual because I was seeking to write in a conversational, informal style—a style heightened by the liberal use of "em" dashes. I would not be using the "em" dash so liberally if I were writing a legal document.

This isn't to say you shouldn't use dashes in formal writing. They're a valuable and, at times, necessary part of your punctuation toolbox. But if you find you've used more than one set of "em" dashes per page of text, you're probably overusing them. Go back to those "dashed" sentences and rework them so that the need for "em" dashes is eliminated or lowered. Doing so will tighten your analysis and conform your writing more to the style legal readers expect but without making it too stiff or formal.

F. Ellipses

Note that "ellipses" is the plural of "ellipsis." You use ellipses—three periods with a space between each one, and all three periods preceded and followed by a space—to indicate an omission of one or more words within a quotation. For example, the quotation "The Court, which has never been tolerant of imprecise writing, was critical of the briefs in this case" can be written in your document as "The Court…was critical of the briefs in this case," with the ellipses indicating the omission of the clause beginning with "which." Your word processor may try to replace the ellipses you type with a condensed version that ignores the correct spacing explained above. Don't let it. If your program makes this substitution, you should disable the appropriate feature.

G. Exclamation Point

This familiar mark should be used with extreme caution, if at all, by legal writers. It's used to indicate extreme emphasis at the end of a sentence—almost always after quoting someone who has made an exclamation of some sort: "Look out behind you! The bear's hungry!" When used, the exclamation point takes the place of the period at the end of a sentence: never write, "Look out!."

An additional use of the exclamation point—to indicate the writer's surprise at something—has crept into usage from the world of chess, where it is an acknowledged mark to indicate a surprising or noteworthy move: "Kt-K 3, ch.!" Unless you're involved in chess litigation, though, you should avoid using this mark. It may be tempting to write, "The defendant's brief was 180 pages long (!) and was devoid of any legal citation," but you should choose your words with such care that your emphasis is achieved without using the exclamation point.

So while the exclamation point has an honorable place in the fiction writer's punctuation arsenal (and even there it's often overused), it has almost no use in legal writing. If you ever find you can't end a sentence without it, however, be sure to place it inside the quotation marks if it emphasizes a quotation.

H. Hyphens

Some experts will tell you not to use the hyphen in place of the "en" dash. This is correct advice, but more technical than most lawyers need.

As a legal writer, you should use hyphens only to indicate a compound modifier: two or more words that gang up on a noun and modify it. For example: a fly-by-night operation; a small-town lawyer; a common-law rule; and so on.

This use of hyphens is important. To see why, consider the following. A client asks you to draw up a contract memorializing an agreement to prepare fifty foot long strips of aluminum for a sculpture. Is this a contract for a specific number of relatively short strips, or is it a less specific agreement to provide numerous long strips?

The location of the hyphen in the following examples changes the meaning: Fifty foot-long strips means a distinct number of strips, each a foot in length; fifty-foot long strips means an indeterminate number of strips, each measuring fifty feet in length.

If you draft the contract without checking for the correct placement of the hyphens, you may draft your client, and yourself, into a problem. Remember that many states construe contracts strictly against the drafter.

The importance of knowing the correct hyphenation of compound modifiers underscores why punctuation really matters in legal writing. If you're not secure about your knowledge of the English language, including punctuation, bad things can happen to you—not just as law students but also as practicing lawyers. Conversely, if you have a secure grasp of English fundamentals, you may well be able to gain an advantage over an opponent who is a less knowing and careful writer.

I. Parentheses

The term "parentheses" (singular = "parenthesis") is the technical name for one type of bracketing mark. Parentheses nearly *always* occur in pairs and look like this: ( ). They're used to set off parts of a sentence that are less important than the remainder of the sentence. There's an example of this usage in the second sentence of the next section—on periods. You also use parentheses to set off shortened forms of terms used immediately before the opening parenthesis: "Widget Company ("Widget")." In addition, you use parentheses to enclose the numbers or letters that designate parts of a list: (a), (b), (c), and so on. And, of course, you use parentheses to set off court and date information from the rest of a citation: *Smith v. Jones*, 123 F.3d 456 (13th Cir. 2005). Note that you should never use just one parenthesis. For example, you shouldn't use a single parenthesis after a number or letter. Avoid "1)" and "a)"—and so on.

J. Period

The period is the most ubiquitous punctuation mark. Almost all sentences (except those with exclamation points or question marks) end in one, and it has at least two other uses as well.

The first of these is to indicate an abbreviation. For example, a person's title—"Mr.," "Dr.," "Prof.,"—are abbreviations of "Mister," "Doctor," and "Professor," respectively, and the abbreviation is indicated by a period. (The other common personal title these days, "Ms.," isn't an abbreviation for a specific, pronounceable word—except, perhaps, "Mizz"—but consistency requires that it end with a period as well.)

The period is also used to indicate enumeration. The subheadings of this section, for example, are enumerated alphabetically— "A.," "B.," and so on. The period shows that the letter is a heading indicator and not simply a stray capital typed onto the page by mistake.

Correctly placing the period in a sentence involving parentheses can appear challenging, but the rule is actually quite simple. If a complete sentence stands alone and is entirely enclosed by parentheses, the period should fall before the closing parenthesis. For example: "(This complete sentence stands alone and is entirely enclosed within parentheses.)" If, on the other hand, only part of a sentence—a phrase, for instance—is enclosed within parentheses, the period falls after the closing parenthesis. For example: "This sentence has only a phrase enclosed within parentheses (and demonstrates the correct placement of the closing period)."

Sentences ending in quotation marks should have the period inserted before the closing quotation marks. For example: "Time drags when you're sitting in a jury assembly area."

And, by the way, although some disagree with this practice, after every period, and after every punctuation mark closing a sentence, you should insert two spaces before beginning the next sentence.

K. Question Mark

There's only one use for the question mark—to indicate a direct question. A direct question is usually enclosed in quotation marks. For example: "Do you know the way to San Jose?" Indirect questions—such as "Dionne Warwick was wondering if you knew the way to San Jose"—don't require question marks.

You should use this mark sparingly because you shouldn't be posing many questions in your writing. In legal writing you answer questions rather than raising them.

Question marks fall inside quotation marks only when they form part of the quotation. For example: "In deposition, the defendant was asked, 'Did you see the light turn green before you drove into the intersection?'" (Note that in the more usual way of writing this sentence—"In deposition, the defendant was asked if she saw the light turn green"—the question is indirect and therefore does not end with a question mark.) When the question is not part of the quotation, the question mark falls outside the quotation marks. For example: "Would the court's decision have been different if, in its own words, 'the proper question had been asked'"? The easiest way to determine the placement of the question mark is to ask who's asking the question—you as the writer, or someone you quote directly in your document. If it's you, the question mark falls outside the quotation marks.

L. Quotation Marks

Quotation marks are used, obviously, to enclose direct quotations. Only use quotation marks to enclose quotations that occur among the sentences of your text. If a quotation is a block quote, it is not enclosed in quotation marks. The requirements for a block quote are usually explained in the citation manual used by your school or office. A general rule is that quotations of more than fifty words should be treated as block quotes.

When an internal quotation lies within a passage you've already quoted, you should use single quotation marks to indicate the internal quotation, even though, in the original, the writer used double quotation marks. For example: "Counsel's comment to the trial judge that he 'didn't know what [he] was doing' merited the contempt sanction it received."

Another use for quotation marks is to enclose a word or a phrase when it is used as a word or a phrase. For example: "In law, the word 'duty' has several different meanings." You should also use quotation marks when defining terms: Widget Company ("Widget").

Finally, quotation marks can be used editorially, to distance the writer from the meaning of the written word or phrase. For example, in a document referring to a court's ruling on the constitutionality of gay "marriage," the use of quotation marks is signaling to the reader that the writer has some reservations about whether "marriage" is a word that can apply in this context.

M. Semicolons

The semicolon—";"—is used primarily to separate the internal divisions within a list when the list as a whole is preceded by a colon. For example: "As a threshold matter, a plaintiff must establish: that the class has enough people; that the class members have claims in common; that the representative's claims are typical of those of the rest of the class members; and that the representative is adequate to represent the class." In such a list, each semicolon should be followed by two spaces, as the example illustrates.

You can also use the semicolon in place of a period when two sentences are short and closely connected. An example: "James was a bad poker player; he always moaned when he was bluffing." If you use a semicolon in this way, it should be followed by two spaces. Also, the first letter of the next sentence is not capitalized.

N. Virgule

The virgule is the mark we usually call the "slash" or the "backslash" and which looks like this: /. Other than its use within Internet URLs, there is only one correct usage of the virgule in formal writing: the separation of numerator from denominator in a fraction.

In the days of typewriters, the fraction for "one-half" could only be typed as "1/2." However, nowadays your computer software can change the typography automatically—from 1/2 to $\frac{1}{2}$, thus indicating that your intended meaning is a fraction rather than a ratio.

Although the virgule is also used occasionally to indicate "per"— as in "that associate bills out at \$250/hour"—this usage is not appropriate in formal legal writing. Also, although the virgule is used in informal writing as a way to indicate the date—6/26/05 for example—this usage, too, is not appropriate for formal legal documents. A final inappropriate usage of the mark is to separate alternatives in a sentence. Although the use of the virgule in phrases like "employer/employee relationship" is creeping into the mainstream, it is not yet accepted in formal legal writing.

Chapter 5

Usage

English is not an easy language. It has a huge vocabulary, and many words that sound similar have different meanings. Some of these differences are obvious and some are subtle, but all are important. In order to be a successful legal writer, you must take these differences into account.

To help you, here's a list of some of the more frequent problem words encountered by lawyers. Some of these are pairs of words frequently confused, and some are words with particularly thorny usage problems. And remember that the following list is only a selection. Whenever you come across a word that causes you a problem, take the time to write down the word, the problem, and the solution. Annotate this manual, or keep your own separate record. Either approach is the surest method of being able to solve the same problem quickly when you next encounter it.

Accept and Except

When you "accept" something, you agree to take it. "Except" usually means "other than." So: "John accepted the good wishes of everyone except James."

Adverse and Averse

These words sound similar and their meanings are close but not identical. "Adverse" means "against": if you're adverse to something you oppose it. "Jane supported the road's construction but James was adverse to the idea." "Averse," by contrast, means "reluctant" or "unwilling." "John was averse to accepting Jane's arguments in support of the road."

Affect and Effect

A tricky couple. Each word has a verb form and a noun form, and "affect" has two different verb meanings, making it crucial that you select the correct word for the meaning you intend:

"Affect" (as a verb) means "to influence or have an effect on something or someone." ("Music deeply affects him.")

"Affect" (as a verb) also means "to pretend." ("She affected not to hear the attorney's question.")

"Affect" (as a noun) means "an emotional response," and it is used most frequently in doctor's clinical notes. ("The patient presented with a flat affect.")

"Effect" (as a noun) means "influence or impact." ("Prozac had no effect on the patient's flat affect.")

"Effect" (as a verb) means "to bring about." ("Litigation has effected a change in the way the company does business.")

As always, you should consider the context of the sentence before choosing which of these words is correct. And because of the possibility of confusion, you should consider whether another word may do the job more effectively.

Aggravate and Irritate

These words are often, mistakenly, used interchangeably. "Irritate" means "to inflame," while "aggravate" means "to worsen." "Mosquito bites irritate the skin, and scratching the bite aggravates the irritation."

All Right

Two words. "All right" is the correct spelling; "alright" is the wrong one. However, usage regarding the correct spelling has begun to change. Microsoft Word's spellchecker, for example, now accepts "alright" as correct. So maybe in a few years "alright" will be generally accepted. But not now.

Alternate and Alternative

"Alternate" as a verb means "to move between one person or thing and another." "John's affections were known to alternate between Jane and Jean." "Alternate" as an adjective means "substituting for another." "If he couldn't steal her jewels, John's alternate plan was to steal Jane's money." "Alternate" as a noun means "a substitute for another." "John's alternate was arrested while trying to steal the tiara." "Alternative" implies a choice between one person or thing and another. "John considered asking Jean to the prom as an alternative to asking Jane."

A Lot

Two words. Try not to use this phrase: "much" is preferable.

Anxious and Eager

Prefer "eager." Save "anxious" for the rare situation where there is some degree of concern—when the actor is troubled by something. So: "John was eager to see Jane," unless "John was anxious to see Jane because he had to explain why she had seen him with Jean."

Apprise and Appraise

These two have completely different meanings. "Apprise" means "to inform." "John was asked to apprise the police of the situation."

It's a fancy word for "tell," so it's preferable that you not use it. "Appraise," on the other hand, means "to evaluate." "John asked Jane if she would appraise the jewels he had stolen."

Assure, Ensure, and Insure

An infamous trap for the unwary. All three words mean the same thing ("to make certain or safe"), but they're used differently, depending on what you're talking about. Use "assure" with people ("John assured Jane her jewels would be safe"), "ensure" with things ("Putting a wedge under the safe door ensured that it would stay open while John stole the jewels"), and "insure" with money ("Jane's jewels were insured for $1,000,000").

As...As

When you are comparing, the correct form is "as...as": "James is *as* big a fool *as* John." Avoid the confusing usage that has crept into commercials recently: "The jewels were worth as much as $1 million *or more*." If the maximum amount of the item's value is $1 million, then "as much as" is correct. If the maximum amount is more than $1 million, use "more than." Another incorrect usage is "as good or better than." The correct form is "as good as, or better than,..." If this seems too wordy, try rephrasing the entire sentence.

Assume and Presume

Here is another example of subtly different meanings. "Assume" implies a degree of doubt: "I assume that John is coming but I'm not sure." "Presume," on the other hand, implies much more certainty, although there's still a degree of doubt: "I presume John is coming unless I hear otherwise."

Bad and Badly

There's an important distinction here that's often misunderstood. "Bad" is an adjective, so it describes a noun. That means it describes a state of being or characterizes a person or thing: "John was a bad man." "Badly," an adverb, modifies a verb and so relates to an action: "John had behaved badly."

Beside and Besides

An example of what a difference one letter can make. "Beside" means "at the side of something." "The bedside table was beside the bed." "Besides," on the other hand, means "in addition to." "Besides the bedside table, there was a rug beside the bed." Because of the potential for confusion, however, avoid using similarly spelled words, each carrying a different meaning, in the same sentence.

Between and Among

Use "between" when referring to two people or things ("The fight was between John and James") and "among" when referring to three or more ("The fight was among five warring factions within the party"). The only exception occurs when you're referring to a group of people or objects that have a close relationship. In that case you should use "between." ("John, James, Jane, and Jean contested the will between them.")

Bi and Semi

Generally, "bi" means "two" and "semi" means "half." So far, so good. "Biannual" means "occurring twice a year." ("That newsletter is a biannual publication.") "Biennial" means "occurring once every two years or every other year." ("The legislature meets biennially.") But "semiannual" can also mean "occurring twice a year." Since many of your readers may confuse the three words, each with its own distinct meaning, the safest approach is just to write what you mean. If you mean "The legislature meets once every two years," write that. If you mean "That newsletter is published twice a year," write that. Each sentence uses more words, but there's no possibility of being misunderstood. If you write "a biannual publication," there's a chance your uninformed reader may think you mean "biennial"—a newsletter published every two years.

Cannot

This is spelled as one word. Don't use "can not."

Compare with and Compare to

Another subtle difference in meaning. "Compare with" implies looking at two persons or things to determine the differences and similarities between them: "The two sets of fingerprints were compared with each other to determine if John alone or both John and James had been at the scene of the crime." "Compared to" shows similarities between two persons or things: "Compared to John, James was just as likely a suspect." If in doubt, you probably mean "compare with," so use that.

Complement and Compliment

As a verb, "complement" means "to complete" or "to support." For example, "John's blue tie complemented his suit." As a noun, it means "a complete number of," as in "When John joined the gang of jewel thieves, it now had a full complement." "Compliment" as a verb means "to praise," as in "Many of the spectators complimented John on his appearance." As a noun, the word means a "praising remark": "John received many compliments on his appearance."

Continually and Continuously

"Continually" means "repeatedly." For example, "Jane was continually checking the school's Web site to see if her grades had been posted." "Continuously," on the other hand, means "without a break." So: "Jane worked on her appellate brief continuously for twenty-four hours." The difference is that "continually" doesn't require the actor to act without a pause: Jane might have checked the Web site every five minutes, but she was doing something else for the rest of the time. But if Jane worked on her brief "continuously," she didn't take any breaks and did nothing other than working on the brief.

Consensus

This word means "general agreement." So saying that something has a "general consensus" is redundant: the word "general" is implied by "consensus."

Criterion and Criteria

Another trap for the unwary. "Criterion" is singular and "criteria" is plural. So if you're just speaking of one thing, use "criterion."

Datum and Data

With this pair, the singular or plural question often rears its ugly head. Just as with "criterion" and "criteria," "datum" is singular and "data" is plural. So if you're referring to just one fact, "datum" should be your choice. If you use "data," you must remember that it's plural. So you should write: "the data *are*," "the data *were*," or "the data *show*," never "the data *is*," "the data *was*," or "the data *shows*."

Decimate

An overused—and misused—word, it actually means "to kill every tenth person ("The Roman centurion decimated the legion by pushing every tenth soldier over a cliff"). Today, the word is often used in circumstances that are much less dramatic: "The football team was decimated by injuries in the first half of the season." But in legal contexts this usage is incorrect. It's also wrong for lawyers to use "decimate" to refer to a percentage other than 10: "The flood decimated almost half of the remaining supplies."

Diagnose

This word is commonly misused. It's the disease that's diagnosed, not the patient. So you should write, "John's condition was diagnosed as kleptomania," not, "John was diagnosed with kleptomania." The misuse of the word has become so common that, in time, the incorrect usage will likely become correct. But that hasn't happened yet—and certainly not in legal contexts.

Differ with and Differ from

Things differ "from" one another; people differ "with" each other. "John's fingerprints differ from James's and John differed with James about the significance of this fact."

Different from and Different than

"Different from" is correct.

Dilemma

If you use this word, it must refer to two choices. So the sentence "John faced a dilemma: should he turn to the left or the right?" is correct. But the sentence "James faced a dilemma: should he tell

Joan, Jean, and Joanna that he had asked Jeanette to the Prom?" is
wrong.

Disinterest and Uninterest

These words (and their adjectival forms "disinterested" and "uninterested," respectively) are often used interchangeably, but there is
a difference. "Disinterest" (or "disinterested") is neutral in conno-
tation: the person has neither interest nor a lack of interest. "Unin-
terest" (or "uninterested"), on the other hand, means "a lack of in-
terest." "John was disinterested in whom James took to the Prom:
he had his own date to worry about." But: "Joan was uninterested
in James's excuses: she would never forgive him for his duplicity in
inviting Jean to the Prom."

Each Other and One Another

There's an easy rule to follow here: use "each other" for two people and "one another" for more than two. So: "John and James had
little respect for each other" and "The five prizewinners shared the
cup between one another for the year."

Either

As a conjunction, "either" must always be followed, even at a distance, by "or." "Either James is a complete idiot or he's a cad."

Everyone and Everybody

The problem here is whether these words—which are used to
refer to at least more than one person and often a large number of
people—should take the singular or plural. And the answer might
surprise you: even though they refer to many people, "everyone"
and "everybody" take the singular. "Everyone *is* happy that John was

caught" and "Everybody *knows* that James is a cad." You probably
know this without thinking about it, but the process of becoming a
lawyer has a way of making you uncomfortable believing anything
you thought you knew before.

Farther and Further

"Farther" implies distance, while "further" means "to a greater
extent" and implies "more." So, for example: "James lived farther
down the street" and "Joan wanted nothing further to do with
James."

Fewer and Less

Another tricky pair. "Fewer" implies a smaller number of more
than one thing, while "less" implies a smaller amount of one thing.
"The company has been sued fewer times this year, and juries have
awarded less money to the plaintiffs."

First and Firstly

Use "first"; don't use "firstly." And don't use first unless there's a
"second." If you disregard the first advice and use "firstly," the rule
about using "first" also applies: you must follow a "firstly" by a "sec-
ondly," and so on. In addition, you should never mix "firstly" with
"second" and "third."

Good and Well

You should use these words in the same way as you use "bad" and
"badly." "Good" is an adjective describing a noun, which can be a
quality, a characteristic, or a state of being: "John was a good thief."
"Well" can be used as an adverb (no, not all adverbs end in "-ly"),

so it can modify a verb and can be used to describe an action: "John stole jewels well and often."

Historic

Be careful before you use "historic" in a sentence. In this era when self-importance reigns, the word is often used to mean "important," as in the sentence: "The baseball team had a historic win over their archrivals last night." But in order to be truly "historic," some person, object, or event must be worthy of being placed in the permanent historical record. The signing of the Declaration of Independence, for example, was a "historic" event.

Hopefully

In spoken English, at least, the battle for the correct usage of "hopefully" has been fought and lost. In written English, however, there's still a chance this word will be used correctly. "Hopefully" is an adverb meaning "with hope": " 'You're not going to sentence me to thirty years are you?' John asked the judge hopefully." This adverb doesn't mean "I hope" or "it is to be hoped." So " 'Hopefully you'll enjoy your cell,' said the judge" is wrong. To make sure you don't misuse this word, don't use it at all.

Hyper and Hypo

The prefix "hyper" means "excessive" or "excessively" and thus suggests "more"; the prefix "hypo" means "less than normal" or "less than normally" and thus suggests "less." These are important prefixes in medicine: it's crucial to know whether someone is hyperglycemic or hypoglycemic, for example. If you're involved in a case where either of these prefixes is used to explain an issue, be sure to double-check everything you write, especially if you dictate your work and have it transcribed. The distinction between "hyper" and "hypo" can be very difficult for a transcriber to hear, and a mistake will render your work contradictory or meaningless.

If and Whether

"If" and "whether" are words that can be used interchangeably—often to indicate alternative conditions or possibilities. For example: "James wondered whether [or if] he should ask Joan or Jean to the Prom." "If," however, is considered informal usage, so you should use "whether" in your legal writing.

Imply and Infer

These two verbs are much misunderstood and much misused. "Imply" connotes a suggestion or a hint ("James implied that John was a thief"), while "infer" suggests the act of deducing something ("The policeman inferred that John was a thief after interrogating James").

In Behalf of and On Behalf of

These two phrases don't mean the same thing at all. "In behalf of" means "in the interest or for the benefit of" and thus suggests support or praise. So: "Jane spoke in behalf of John at his sentencing." "On behalf of" means "acting as agent or representative of" and can suggest instead of: "John asked Jane to the prom on behalf of James, who was too shy."

In To and Into

Confusing these two can lead to much embarrassment. "Into" indicates only motion ("John was told to get into his cell") and transformation ("His time in prison changed John from a career criminal into a model citizen"). In contexts other than motion or transformation, use "in to": "The jury came in to deliver John's verdict."

Irregardless

A word that looks like a standard English word but isn't. It is used only in informal speech—as if it had the same meaning as "regardless." Some writers mistakenly believe it is standard usage—perhaps because the two initial letters make it look "fancier." Even if "irregardless" were acceptable, the addition of "ir-" would give it a meaning opposite to "regardless." So use "regardless," never "irregardless," in standard written or spoken English.

Irony

One of the more commonly misused words in our times. Something is "ironic" if it means the opposite of what's being said: " 'I really want to go to jail,' John said ironically." So in the sentence "It's ironic that John was captured robbing Jane's house because he was going to ask her to the prom the next day," the word "ironic" is misused. John's capture and intention may be surprising, or coincidental, but they are not ironic.

Lay and Lie

The verb "lay" means "to place something": "Before handcuffing him, the policeman asked John to lay his burglar's tools down." The verb "lie" means "to recline": "After being handcuffed, John was told to lie on the floor until the policeman could determine he had no concealed weapons." "Lay" is also the past tense of "lie," which has caused no end of confusion. In the context of reclining, here are three sentences showing the use of "lie" in the present, past, and future tenses, respectively: "John lies on the floor. Last night, he lay on the floor. If the policeman doesn't tell him to get up, he will be lying there tomorrow as well." "Lay" never means "to recline" in the present tense. So don't say or write, "Just lay down there." Instead, use "lie."

Like and As

The word "like" in informal usage has become a universal sentence opener in conversation ("Like, what's your problem?"), but I fervently hope you will never use "like" in this way in your writing or in oral arguments in court. Judges don't respond well to "Like, may it please the court."

In formal usage, there are specific rules for whether you use "like" or "as." Use "as" if it's followed by a verb. If the verb has already appeared in the sentence, use "like." For example: "As anyone would do when being arrested, John trembled" and "John trembled like a leaf in the wind when he was arrested." Reversing this usage can make your writing sound faintly Biblical: "John trembled as a leaf in the wind when he was arrested." Such quaintness is not what lawyers are looking for.

Literal

Another candidate for most misused word these days. "Literal" means "actual" or "precise." "John stole literally hundreds of jewels" means that John has stolen more than 200 jewels ("hundreds" means "more than 100, with 100 as the base unit"). So if John actually stole 90 jewels, or 190, in the sentence above he hasn't stolen "literally" hundreds, and thus the word "literally" is misused. A worse misuse occurs when "literally" is used to mean "metaphorically," as in the sentence, "John was literally dead on his feet after a long night of robbery." The sentence is intended to suggest that John was tired, but its "literal" meaning is that John's life was over and that he is, and will remain forever, clinically dead.

Loath and Loathe

Here's another example of a big difference in meaning caused by a difference in one letter. "Loath" means "unwilling" ("James was loath to invite Joan to the Prom"), while "loathe" is one of the strongest of words meaning "dislike" ("Joan loathed James for not inviting her to the Prom").

Loose and Lose

Here's yet another difference in one letter—leading to yet another confusion between two entirely different words. "Loose" (an adjective) means "not secure," whereas "lose" (a verb) means "to no longer have something." So: "John's loose button might fall and activate the sensors around the safe. If that happens, he might lose the chance to steal the jewels." This difference in usage is especially tricky because it's easy to type, by accident, an incorrect "loose" (an extra "o") rather than a correct "lose." The computer's automatic spell-checker won't catch the mistake because "loose" is a word correctly spelled.

May and Might

A tricky pair—with three potential problems in usage. To explain the easier usage first, "may" and "might" can be used to describe varying degrees of probability. "May" suggests a greater likelihood than "might." So "John might get away with stealing the jewels" implies that his action is possible but not likely, while "John may get caught if he keeps stealing jewels" implies that his action is not only possible but more likely.

A second problem in usage can occur when you realize that both "may" and "might" can be used in the past tense. The sentences "Joan may have been disappointed not to have been asked to the Prom" and "Joan might have been disappointed not to have been asked to the Prom" are both equally correct. But if there's another past tense verb in the sentence, only "might" is correct: "Jean was concerned that Joan might have been disappointed not to have been invited to the Prom."

A third, and final, problem in usage can occur when "might" and "may" have completely different meanings. Compare "Asking Joan to the prom might have prevented John from a life of crime" (meaning that John *didn't* ask Joan and that he *did* enter into a life of crime) to "Asking Joan to the Prom may have prevented John from a life of crime" (meaning that John *did* ask Joan to the Prom and that he *didn't* enter into a life of crime). Once again, as these three thorny usage problems indicate, you should know the precise meaning of every word you use, in context, before submitting your work.

Medium and Media

Here is another singular or plural usage problem, like "datum" and "data." "Medium" is singular and "media" is plural. "Joan's chosen medium is watercolor. This detail is often overlooked by the media when they interview her."

Memorandum and Memoranda

"Memorandum" is the singular form; "memoranda" (not "memorandums") is the plural form.

Neither

Just as "either" as a conjunction can't exist in a sentence without "or," "neither" as a conjunction can't exist without "nor." And just as with "either," "nor" needn't follow directly after "neither." "Neither John, who is serving a thirty-year sentence for jewel theft, nor James, who is going with Jean, will be accompanying Joan to the Prom." Never partner "neither" with "or" or "either" with "nor."

None

Confusingly, "none" can be singular or plural depending on its context. If followed by a singular noun, "none" is singular as well. If it's followed by a plural noun, it's plural. So: "None of the meal was edible" or "None of John's meals were edible."

Only

The way this word is used points out the importance of word order. Incorrect usage of "only" isn't always immediately evident, but its placement in a sentence can cause the meaning of the sentence to change. The usage rule is that "only" should be placed immediately before the word it modifies. What this means can (I hope) be seen clearly by example. Consider "John only steals jewels" and "John steals only jewels." By placing "only" before "steals," I'm saying that all John does is steal jewels; he has no other activity in life. But by placing "only" before "jewels," I'm saying that John won't steal money, or paintings, or pets—just jewels. And "Only John steals jewels" means that no one else is a jewel thief.

On To and Onto

As with "in to" and "into," these two similar-looking words have different meanings. "Onto" means "on top of." If you mean something other than "on top of," use "on to." So: "James placed the prom queen's crown onto Jean's head" whereas "After James put the crown in his bag, he moved on to steal the necklace as well."

Oral and Verbal

An important distinction for lawyers to note here. "Oral" means "spoken" but "verbal" means "consisting of words." "Verbal" is often misused to mean *only* "spoken." So an oral contract is a spoken agreement, but a verbal contract can be spoken or written.

Ought and Ought To

"Ought to" is correct when you write or speak in the positive: "John ought to know better." "Ought" works when you write or speak in the negative: "John ought not have stolen the jewels."

Note that the "to" is still present in the negative sentence; it's just implied rather than stated: "John ought not (to) have stolen the jewels."

Phenomenon and Phenomena

Another singular or plural issue. "Phenomenon" is singular and "phenomena" is plural.

Presently

"Presently" doesn't mean what it sounds as if it should mean: "at the present." Instead, it means "at some indeterminate time in the future." So if you write, "The bill is presently under consideration by a House committee" and mean that the committee is considering the bill at the present, you are misusing "presently." Instead, you should write, "The bill is at present under consideration by a House committee." One giveaway for the misuse of "presently" is its use in the present tense. Because "presently" means "in the future," it should only appear in the context of the future: "James will presently make a decision about whom to ask to the prom."

Quiet and Quite

The displacement of the "e" here can make a big difference in the sentence's meaning. "Quiet" means "peaceful" and "quite" means either "completely" ("John was quite sure he wouldn't ask Joan to the prom") or "to a degree" ("John thought Joan's jewels were quite attractive, so he stole them").

Statue and Statute

These words involve one of the most common spelling mistakes made by lawyers and not caught by electronic spell-checkers. Leaving out the final "t" in "statute" makes the writer look sloppy and makes the sentence incomprehensible: "John laughed in the face of the burglary statue."

That and Which

One classic problem in English usage is still the question of whether the relative pronouns "that" or "which" should come at the beginning of a subordinate (or, strictly speaking, relative) clause. The problem still occurs perhaps because the classic explanation is not especially easy to understand: *That* is a defining relative pronoun, whereas *which* is a nondefining one.

Here are two simpler explanations. First, if the relative pronoun is preceded by a comma, use "which," and if it isn't, use "that." Second, if you can leave out the relative clause and not change or lose the meaning of the sentence, use "which"; otherwise, use "that." If in doubt, use "that," because it's correct about 90 percent of the time.

Examples may simplify these already simplified explanations. "John's profession, which was that of a jewel thief, was illegal." The sentence would work without the relative clause "which was that of a jewel thief." It would then read just, "John's profession was illegal," and the meaning of the sentence hasn't changed. John's profession is still illegal, whatever it is. So because (a) the relative pronoun is preceded by a comma, and (b) leaving out the relative clause doesn't change the meaning of the sentence, "which" is the correct relative pronoun. Compare the sentence above to "The jewels that John stole were valuable." There's no comma preceding the relative pronoun, and if you take out the relative clause "that John stole," the meaning of the sentence has changed. The jewels are valuable in both sentences, but if you take out the clause beginning with "that," the fact that the jewels have been stolen is missing from the sentence. So "that" is the correct choice.

Their, There, and They're

The usage issues here aren't as tricky as they may at first appear. "Their" is the possessive form of "they": "John and James believed that their charm would get them out of trouble." By contrast, "there" means "in that place": "John put the jewels down over there." "They're" is a contraction meaning "they are": "John and James aren't charming: they're jewel thieves."

Unique

"Unique" means "the one and only." You can't qualify "unique". Something can't be "almost unique" or "really unique"; it's either unique or it isn't. Just as one can't be "a little bit dead," one can't be "a little bit unique."

Utilize

This word is a pretentious way of saying "use." Try always to avoid using fancier-sounding words to say something simple. We lawyers use pretentious words all the time, probably because we think that the fancier something sounds, the more likely someone is to believe it. In fact, the opposite is probably true. So don't "utilize a graphite/carbon-based scribal tool to practice the calligraphic arts," just "use a pencil to write."

Chapter 6

General Formatting Issues

Having talked about some of the elements of style, let's now turn to form. And although thinking about form—the appearance of written words on a page—is one of the humblest of the many things legal writers do, it's still crucially important. You can have a brilliant analysis and still not be taken seriously, or even read, if your work doesn't conform to your reader's expectations of how information should be presented.

In fact, until your brief is accepted for filing by the court, the form of your document is the most important thing about it. A weak argument, poorly supported and badly written, will beat the most brilliant legal argument ever made if the weak argument is properly formatted according to the court's rules and is therefore accepted for filing by the clerk's office at the courthouse, and if the brilliant argument is improperly formatted according to the rules and is therefore rejected by the clerk's office.

The importance clerks place on properly formatted documents can't be overstated. As gatekeepers to the court, they, and not the judges, oversee the filing process, part of which concerns the correct rules for formatting. So until your document has passed the clerk's office's scrutiny, the clerk is the most important reviewer of your document.

The clerk's pivotal role makes local formatting rules extraordinarily important. Don't treat any of them as trivial or irrelevant. In addition, please remember that anything I say here is trumped by jurisdictional rules, whether those of a court, your law firm, or your legal writing teacher. What I write here will help you produce generic, acceptable documents as long as you are writing for a forum without its own formatting requirements for documents. If the person or court for whom you're writing has special requirements, follow them carefully and ignore what you read below.

A. Paper

Use plain, white 8.5-by-11-inch paper unless you're told to use a different kind or size of paper. Some courts require pleadings to be filed using legal-sized paper; others require double red margins; others require documents with line numbers for text; and still others require blue backing on all documents filed with the court. If you're working in a law firm, be sure to check the formatting requirements of the attorneys with whom you work and follow them. Some attorneys, for instance, prefer documents on legal-sized paper, and some prefer to read copies of documents on colored paper so as not to confuse an original with a copy. Careful adherence to each idiosyncratic requirement will single you out as a legal writer who pays attention to detail, and that is perhaps the best compliment you'll get as a junior lawyer.

The paper you use should be designed for the type of printer you use. So if you're using an ink jet printer, use paper intended for ink jets, and if you're using a laser printer, use paper for that. Don't use expensive resume-style paper in your legal-writing assignments unless you're told to do so: it costs more than necessary and likely won't impress anyone.

B. Printing

Virtually all legal documents these days should be prepared on computers and printed, with the exception of some forms that still must be typed. You should not write anything on any document, except for an assignment specifically requiring you to submit something in handwriting. The only exception to this is your required signature on a document.

C. Font and Size

All printed assignments should use Times New Roman font, and should use 12- point type for all text, including footnotes. Your computer will likely have 10-point type set as default for footnotes, but you should either change this on your finished document or change the default settings on your computer. A 12-point type will make your footnotes more readable.

Times New Roman is a standard, ordinary font. Many other fonts are just as acceptable, but Times New Roman has become the most-used font in the legal community and there's no reason for you to swim against the tide. You want the content of your documents to be memorable, not their textual appearance.

D. Margins

Your documents should have top, bottom, left, and right margins each of one inch. You can set such margins using your word processor's page setup menu. Occasionally you will indent text (usually the beginnings of paragraphs), and you will indent both the left and right margins of block quotes by 0.5 inches. But the basic setup of your page should reflect the one-inch margins that are the default settings of most word processing programs.

E. Spacing

As a general rule, your documents should be double-spaced. It makes your text easier to read, and it gives the reader room to make notes or editorial changes if necessary. There are, though, some exceptions to this rule. Block quotes, for example, are single-spaced, as are headings of more than one line. Itemized text—for instance, text after bullets—is also single-spaced.

F. Page Numbers

All your documents should have page numbers as a matter of course. For memoranda and briefs, page numbers should be placed at the bottom center of each page, and the page number should be omitted from the first page. Your word processing software should allow you to set up the correct page numbering with ease. (The page numbering format is different for correspondence—which will be explained in the section on correspondence.)

G. Indents

Each paragraph in the main body of your text should be indented 0.5 inches from the left margin, except for text in a block quote. Even if the block quote starts at the beginning of a paragraph, the quoted text should not be indented. Moreover, if the block quote runs beyond one paragraph in the original, the text of the second paragraph of your quote should still not be indented. Instead, you should double-space at the end of the first paragraph and begin the second paragraph using the global 0.5 inch indent you've used for the entire block quote.

The reason for this exception is simple. We indent paragraph beginnings to tell the reader we've moved from one body of information to the next. There's no need to do this, though, when we've double-spaced within a block quote: the reader already has the necessary visual clue.

H. Spacing after Punctuation

This next point is controversial because it's old-fashioned. You should type two spaces, not just one, after periods, colons, and semicolons. This was the rule for typewritten documents, and many argue that it's no longer necessary because word processors and printers allow us to create neater and more uniform documents than were possible in the days of the typewriter. Some even argue that typing two spaces after these three punctuation marks makes a document less readable. But typing two spaces serves the same function as the indent at the beginning of a paragraph: it gives the reader a visual clue as to where one group of information ends and another begins. So the technique, though old-fashioned, helps the reader navigate through your document.

Moreover, judges and law firm partners tend not to have read the latest word on publishing aesthetics or document preparation and may expect you to follow the two-spaces convention. Although it may not coincide with current thinking about best formatting practices, following the two-spaces convention is the safest approach until it is so archaic it is considered odd. It will likely be a long time before that happens, however.

I. Omissions

When quoting from text, you should indicate omissions by using one of two methods. For omissions within a regular quote, use three spaced ellipsis dots; for omissions spanning a paragraph break within a block quote, double space, use three spaced asterisks (spaced one inch, or two tab stops, apart), then double space again. (There are two exceptions to these methods, and both will be discussed in the section on insertions into text.)

The first method looks like this: "When omitting text...within a regular quote, use three spaced ellipsis dots." When the omission occurs at the end of a sentence, there are four spaced ellipsis dots—three spaced ellipsis dots and a period: "Omissions are marked by ellipsis dots...." The same rule applies when you've omitted an entire sentence: a period marking the end of the sentence, then a space, then three spaced ellipsis dots indicating the omitted sentence.

The punctuation for the block quote omission looks like this:

> This is the first portion of a block quote, although it contains an insufficient number of words to function as a block quote under the rules expressed in both the Bluebook and the ALWD Manual.
>
>   * * *
>
> This is the second part of the block quote, after the asterisks marking the omission of text that spans over a paragraph break.

Your quotes should be exact, so it's important that when you omit something from a quote, the reader is left in no doubt as to how that omission has been made.

J. Insertions

For the same reason, it's important that your reader know when you've inserted text into a quote. You do this by placing the insertion within square brackets. For example, when you want to use the quote to start a sentence, but the text you've selected to quote begins in the middle of the quote, you insert a capital letter at the beginning of the text selected from the quote and enclose that capital letter in square brackets. It's simpler to show this than it is to describe it. Suppose the sentence you want to quote reads, "Although the method of inserting text can readily be explained, the use of examples makes the point more clearly." If you want to omit the first clause and quote only the second, and at the same time begin your own sentence with it, you would write the following: "[T]he use of examples makes the point more clearly."

The above is the first of the exceptions to showing omitted text with spaced ellipsis points I mentioned in Section I. There's no need to show the omission here, because the square brackets tell your reader there's been an omission. If, however, you *don't* want to start your own sentence with the quoted text, then the ellipsis points are required, and once again, "...the use of an example makes this point clearer." The reason for this should be obvious: when the quote begins without an inserted capital letter, there is no alternative visual clue to the reader showing the omission, so the ellipsis points are necessary.

You can also use square brackets to show substituted text—the second exception to using ellipsis dots to show omitted text. Suppose the sentence you want to quote reads: "The Court finds James to be liable for John's injuries." You don't really care about James and John; what's important to you is that the defendant was found liable for the plaintiff's injuries. So you could substitute procedural designations for names: "The Court finds [defendant] liable for [plaintiff's] injuries." Once again, you've omitted text—in this case the names—but no ellipsis dots are necessary because you've substituted information and you've made that clear to the reader with your use of square brackets.

K. Mistakes

Just like everyone else, lawyers (and even judges) make mistakes in legal documents. When quoting from a document with a mistake, you want to be sure to quote correctly but you don't want your reader to think that *you* made the mistake.

There are two techniques you can use to accomplish this. First, you can reproduce the mistake exactly and then insert "sic" in square brackets immediately after the mistake. For example: "In this brief, the word "breif" [sic] is misspelled." Second, you can spell the word correctly but place it within square brackets because you are inserting the correctly spelled word and omitting the incorrect spelling. So: "In this brief, the word "[brief]" is misspelled."

Both of these techniques are correct, and they can be used interchangeably. But they can be viewed very differently by the reader. Using "sic" is a forceful way of pointing out that the original writer made a mistake, that you know about the mistake, and that you don't want your reader to think you'd be so foolish as to make that mistake yourself. Simply correcting the spelling, and showing that correction by use of an inserted word in square brackets, is a gentler way of conveying the same impression.

However, you should not restrict yourself to one technique. For example, sometimes you may want to point out to a court that your opponent's brief is such a poor piece of work that it even contains misspellings. In this instance, using "sic" may well be appropriate. There are other occasions, though, when you might want to quote from a judge's previous opinion without forcefully indicating that the judge made a technical mistake. In this situation, inserting the correctly spelled word in square brackets may be a safer alternative.

The point here is that everything you place in a document conveys meaning, even something as simple as an indicated misspelling. You must constantly make sure that the meaning you're conveying is the one you want to the reader to get.

L. Symbols

As lawyers, we're fortunate that we don't need to learn an entire vocabulary of signs and symbols. There are two symbols, though, that we use often: the section symbol—§—and the paragraph symbol—¶. These symbols, along with a bewildering array of additional ones, can be found in most word processing programs. For ease of use, you should create keyboard shortcuts that allow you to insert these symbols into your work without recourse to the mouse. Handwriting these symbols into your documents is not acceptable.

M. Emphasis

When we speak we're able to use our voices and bodies to impart emphasis to certain words and phrases within our sentences. We do this in many ways—volume, speed, tone, and even gesture (although please avoid those twitching fingers, often known as "air quotes," to symbolize quotation marks). But in writing, we have only the words on the page: no variation in volume is possible without resorting to tricks like changing the font size, something you should never do in a formal legal document. So we often resort to symbolic emphasis to get the same point across: we don't *need* to use such emphasis, but it makes us feel that our writing is clearer somehow, more akin to the way we speak. In that last sentence, for example, the emphasis placed on "need" by the use of italics simulated vocal emphasis.

In informal writing, italics (or another form of emphasis) is fine, even though it loses its effect if it's overused. But in formal writing—especially in legal writing—typographical emphasis should be used rarely, if at all. The words we choose to make our point should be sufficient. If we feel a need to emphasize the words (with italics, say), we have likely used the wrong words to indicate our point.

This doesn't mean that your first drafts can't use forms of emphasis. At that point in the drafting process, you may want to set your volume of voice by emphasizing some words. Techniques of emphasis should serve to remind you of the important points in your document, but you should seek to eliminate italics and other methods of emphasis in the second and subsequent drafts. Once the editing process starts, and the analysis has become relatively stable, you can work on refining the points you're making and that means considering the words most appropriate for the main points of the analysis. Once that's done, usually there's no need for using techniques of emphasis: your careful choice of language highlights everything that needs to be emphasized. But such meticulous care in choosing the appropriate words can be dangerous to the ultimate outcome of your work if you're unsure of how much time you'll have to edit your work, or if you're not confident that your editing technique is sound.

The one exception to this caution on using techniques of emphasis occurs when you're using someone else's words in a quotation. When there's something in the quote the reader might miss, or if your opponent has made a particularly significant concession, you might want to emphasize that portion of the quote—but never more than once on a page and, ideally, only once in an entire document. That way, emphasis retains its significance. If you italicize every second line, for example, italics quickly become just an annoying quirk, and any chance you have of impressing the reader with the significance of a particular line or word is gone.

If you emphasize your own text, there's no need to explain that you've added the emphasis. If, however, you emphasize something someone else has written, you must place, in parentheses and at the end of the citation, the words "emphasis added." And if the passage you're quoting was already emphasized, you have to indicate that as well: type "emphasis in original."

N. Block Quotes

You should be very cautious when using block quotes. They are, by definition, large chunks of text you didn't write; they're visually unappealing and difficult to read; and they disrupt the flow of your writing. Although every legal writer has to include a block quote occasionally, you should consider carefully whether you can convey the point contained in that quote in a more succinct and personal way.

To indicate a block quote, you single space the text to be quoted, set it apart from the rest of the text by a double space at both the top and the bottom of the quote, then indent the whole by 0.5 inches (one tab stop) from both the left and right margins. The block quote is not enclosed in quotation marks, and the citation to the quote is placed in the main body of text—in other words, not in the block quote itself.

Here's an example of what a block quote and citation should look like:

> When block quoting, the writer should be careful to count the necessary number of words. If the quote has fewer than fifty words, there's no need to put the reader through the unpleasant business of reading a solid block of words. If, on the other hand, the quote is crucial, and can't be paraphrased or otherwise reworded to eliminate the necessity of direct quotation, it's important to follow the rules regarding block quotation scrupulously. It's particularly important to place the citation to the quotation on the next line of normal text and not to place it within the block of text.

Ian Gallacher, *A Form and Style Manual for Lawyers* (Carolina Academic Press 2005).

Note that the double space which sets the block quote apart from the text is a single carriage return for text formatted as double-spaced; but the double space can also be indicated by a single carriage return for text formatted as single-spaced. This seems logical, but block quotes are often mistakenly set off by two double spaces because of confusion on this point. If your text looks like the example, you'll be fine.

O. Justification

Set your word processor so that the margins are only aligned left. Do not use justified margins in your documents. Justified text contains spacing distortions necessary to get the right hand margin to align itself properly and can therefore distort the appearance of your document. Also, left-aligned documents are easier to read.

P. Default Settings

Your word processor will likely try to take control of your document at some points during the drafting process. Sometimes this attempt can be benign. If your computer automatically corrects words you misspell frequently, for example, it can save you time during the spell-checking process.

Indeed, if there are some words you know you misspell often, you can add them to the autocorrect feature and it will correct the misspelling as soon as it occurs. And if there are some lengthy words or even phrases you type often, you can add a meaningless letter combination—"zq" for example—to the autocorrect feature and instruct it to replace the combination with the desired phrase. For example, a typed "zq" could automatically become "the Well Designed and Manufactured Widget Company."

But at other times, your word processing program's default settings are less welcome. One example—a program's default omission of the required spaces between the three ellipsis dots necessary to show a textual omission—has already been discussed. Other default settings are equally troublesome: the tendency to turn the letter "c" in brackets—"(c)"—into the copyright symbol—"©"; the automatic capitalization of letters following periods, which can wrongly capitalize the versus symbol in case citations so that *Smith Corp. v. Jones*, for example, becomes *Smith Corp. V. Jones*; and some word processors' default addition of two spaces after every period, not just the ones ending sentences, which can turn a correct citation form—"325 A.2d 425"—into an incorrect one—"325 A. 2d 425."

These errors are not caught by the spell-checking or grammar-checking features of your word processor and must therefore be discovered and eliminated by you after careful proofreading of your document. When you find your word processor making one of these changes, change the default setting immediately to avoid the problem. If, in its original default setting, your word processor made the mistake once, it will make the same mistake again. And next time you may not catch it.

Q. Numbers

There are many different opinions on how to treat numbers in text. Much more important than the reason for each of these opinions is that you adopt and stick to a consistent system. The simplest option is to spell out whole numbers between one and nine and use numerals for 10 and higher. For decimals, use numerals. An exception: if a number higher than nine occurs at the beginning of a sentence, you should spell out the number. For example, don't write, "12 percent of the population in this county lives below the poverty level." Instead, write, "Twelve percent of the population...." If spelling out the number results in an awkward sentence, rephrase the sentence so that the number is placed elsewhere. Instead of writing, "Twelve point five percent....," write, "Of the population in this county, 12.5 percent...."

R. Headings

Headings are a matter of formatting style that drives lawyers and law students crazy. Heading formats aren't substantive, and yet it takes a lot of care and attention to get them right. In part, this happens because there's no standard way of formatting headings. There are just too many options, and being spoiled for choice is not always helpful.

The answer is to pick a consistent approach and stick with it. The following suggestions will make your headings consistent and well-structured. And if you don't like the results, or if the teacher, lawyer, or court for whom you're writing has special formatting requirements, you should change these suggestions in order to produce a consistent result that meets these requirements or your preferences.

i. Numbering Headings

First, not every heading gets a number. In memoranda, only the sections contained in the "discussion" or "analysis" section get numbers, and in briefs, only the sections contained within the "argument" section get numbers.

ii. Order of Heading Identifiers

Each principal section of your analysis (the content of the "discussion" or "argument" sections) begins with an uppercase Roman numeral, followed by a period: I.; II.; III.; IV.; V.; VI.; VII.; VIII.; IX.; and X..If you need to go beyond 10 (X.), of course, you can. If you have that many principal arguments, though, you might want to rethink your analysis.

Each subsection, sub-subsection, and so on, has an identifying mark in the following order: capital letter, followed by a period (A., B., C., and so on); Arabic numeral, followed by a period (1., 2., 3., and so on); lowercase letter, followed by a period (a., b., c., and so on); lowercase Roman numeral, followed by a period (i., ii., iii., and so on). If you need more identifiers (and again, you might want to reconsider your analysis if you do), you can use double letters, usually lowercased, followed by a period (aa., bb., cc., and so on).

iii. Formatting Heading Identifiers

Section headings ("Question Presented," "Discussion," "Argument," and so on) are centered, but have no identifiers. The principal sections of your analysis should be indented 0.5 inches from the left margin (one tab stop). Each subsequent subheading (and sub-subheading, and so on) should be indented one further tab stop.

This sounds much more complicated than it looks, so let's see the whole outline in practice. In the following example, other formatting issues have been ignored to concentrate only on the locations of the various headings:

Argument

I. Principal Heading
   A. First Subheading
      1. First Sub-subheading
         a. First Sub-sub-subheading
            i. First Sub-sub-sub-subheading
               aa. First Sub-sub-sub-sub-sub heading
II. Second Principal Heading
   A. Second Subheading
      1. Second sub-subheading
         a. Second sub-sub-subheading

And so on. The only mildly complicated part of this is remembering how many tab stops are required for a particular subheading. Don't worry about this requirement during the drafting stage. Only consider it when all the drafting is over and you proofread what you've drafted.

iv. Formatting Headings

This takes a little more care. Section headings get the full treatment: all capital letters, bold type, and underlining. And in subheadings (the ones that are indented from the left margin), each initial letter of each word is capitalized, no matter the length of the word. This is perhaps different from what you were taught—that articles, conjunctions, and prepositions aren't given initial capital letters.

Subheadings of more than one line should be single-spaced. If your subheading is more than one line long, you should make sure its text forms a block, each line approximately the same length. This may require some tinkering (during the editing stage) and you may not be able to create an exact block. Don't worry about this, but if the lines are uneven, try to make the last line longer than the previous ones—an attempt which may seem strange.

Subheadings should be underlined. For subheadings consisting of many lines, only the last (the longest) line should be underlined. Double space between each subheading.

Like the previous one, this formatting issue sounds more complicated than it is and an illustration (found on the page opposite) should make it clearer. Note that the illustration contains only the first portion of the argument. If the sample contained a full series of headings, the first principal heading (I.) would be followed by at least one more principal heading, and the first subheading (A.) would be followed by at least one more subheading.

Note that the formatting of these headings is not the same as that of a table of contents. We'll discuss tables in the next chapter. For now, though, if you're used to seeing tables of contents, the above organization may look strange probably because you don't usually see headings like these without text separating them.

<u>ARGUMENT</u>

I. Standards For Review Of A
Class Certification Motion

    A. <u>The Class Does Not Meet The Requirements Of Rule 23(a)</u>

        1. <u>The Class Is Not So Large That Joinder Is Impractical</u>

        2. The Claims Of The Proposed Class
Representatives Do Not Raise Common
Issues Of Law Or Fact And Are Not Typical
<u>Of The Claims Of The Other Proposed Class Members</u>

        3. The Proposed Class Representatives
Are Not Adequate To Represent
<u>The Claims Of Putative Class Members</u>

            a. The Proposed Class Contains Deep
<u>Divisions Which Cannot Be Reconciled</u>

            b. Class Counsel Have An
<u>Irreconcilable Conflict Of Interest</u>

                i. Rule 23(a)(4) Applies To Class
<u>Counsel As Well As Representatives</u>

                ii. Attorneys May Not Engage
In Representation For One
Client Which Conflicts With
<u>The Representation Of Another</u>

            c. Two Proposed Class Representatives
Do Not Meet Rule 23 (a)(4)'s Threshold
<u>Requirements And Are Per Se Inadequate</u>

            d. Each Individual Proposed Class
Representative Is Inadequate
<u>To Protect The Interests Of The Class</u>

                i. <u>Ms. Scarlet</u>

                ii. <u>Mr. Blue</u>

                iii. <u>Mr. Puce</u>

                iv. <u>Ms. Green</u>

There's another important thing to remember about headings. You should not have just one subheading indicator; you should have at least two. What this means in practice is that you can't have, say, an organization like this:

I.

    A.

II.

If there's a I, there should be at least a II; and if there's an A, there should be at least a B. This rule also applies to subheading indicators. If you find you've drafted your analysis so that it has just one subheading indicator, you should revise your analysis.

S. Defining Terms

Lawyers must often refer frequently to an entity or a document with a lengthy name. In litigation or contracts involving an organization called Well Designed and Manufactured Widget Company, for example, it is important that this entity be properly and accurately identified each time its name comes up. The same is true if you refer to The Supreme Court of Eastern Dakota Standing Committee on Rules of Practice and Procedure, Minutes of the Meeting of Standing Committee on Rules of Practice and Procedure (Mar. 11–12, 1983). But typing these long names each time you refer to them takes up a lot of valuable space and unnecessarily distracts your reader's attention.

The solution is to define these terms. To do so, choose a short form of the term you're defining. In the case of the organization, you would probably choose the short form it has adopted, or create your own short version — "Widget," for example. Your choice should make sense in the context of the document you're drafting, and it should be immediately clear to the reader that you're using a defined term to refer to a related longer name or phrase. In the Rules Committee example, if you're only referring to one set of minutes in your document, you could adopt "Standing Committee Minutes" as your short form. If, however, you're referring to the minutes from a variety of different states, you might want to use "Eastern Dakota Standing Committee Minutes." If you're quoting from a variety of meetings of the same Committee, you might want to use "March 1983 Standing Committee Minutes."

Once you've adopted the short form for the longer name, the format for defining the name is straightforward. Immediately after the first appearance of the name, place the short form of the name in parentheses and quotation marks. Your short form should have an initial capital letter (or letters) in order to set it apart from the normal usage of the same word in your document. For example, if you want to use a short name to refer to the Well Designed and Manufactured Widget Company, the definition should look like this: "In this case, the defendant Well Designed and Manufactured Widget Company ("Widget") caused John Smith's injuries and should therefore be found liable on all counts of the Complaint."

The reason for the capitalization is simple. If you don't differentiate between the defined term ("Widget") and its normal usage (the widget which "Widget" manufactures), any time you use the word widget without the capital in your document, the reader will have to determine from the context whether you are referring to the company or to the product it makes. Your failure to capitalize violates the principle that the defined entity be properly and accurately identified in the document. Any confusion can be readily avoided with the use of the initial capital letter.

You don't need any explanatory phrase, such as "hereinafter referred to as": the placing of the term in parentheses and quotation marks is a sufficient signal. Occasionally, you may want to place an article before the defined term. If so, the article should be in the parentheses but not in the quotation marks — (the "Defendant").

However, you should only adopt this practice when clarity demands the use of the article.

In order to be consistent, once you define a term you should always use the defined form when referring to that term. In the Widget Company example, once you have defined the name of the company as "Widget," you shouldn't later refer to the company as "Well Designed and Manufactured Widget Company." Once again, such usage would make the meaning unclear: the reader might wonder if this entity is intended to be different from the entity you've been identifying as "Widget."

Generally, you shouldn't use a party's legal relationship to litigation as a defined term. Although the Widget Company may be the defendant in litigation, it's usually much clearer to use "Widget" as the defined term than "Defendant." This is especially true in appellate litigation: the federal rules of appellate procedure specifically forbid the use of the terms "appellant" and "appellee."[1] And even in cases where the federal rules don't apply, the better practice is to use a party's name wherever possible as the defined term.

One final word about defined terms. Just because we can define terms doesn't always mean that we should. Many legal documents end up looking as if they're written more in code than in English, with groups of letters and cryptic single words standing for names and phrases. Ironically, this technique—designed to make a document easier to follow—can make the document almost impossible to understand. So if you have a long and cumbersome name that will appear throughout the document and that can readily be reduced to a shorter term, you should consider defining that name with a shorter one. But you should use this technique sparingly and only when it's necessary.

---

1. Fed. R. App.P. 28(d).

T. Lists

Lawyers often have to deal with information that is, or could be, itemized. Whenever possible, it's usually best to present this information typographically as a list. Lists allow the reader to understand the organizational principle at work and to follow the analysis more closely.

When presenting information in a list—or in tabulated form, which is the fancier way of saying the same thing—you should keep some requirements in mind. First, if the list falls after a colon, each item in the list should make as much sense as if it were written to replace the colon. "Defendants should prevail because: (a) the law is on their side; (b) the facts are on their side; and (3) their attorney is smarter." If the word "because" were inserted between "(3)" and "their attorney," the list-sentence would be illogical because of the circular reasoning in the repetition "….because:…(3) because…." Second, list only items that group together naturally. A list that looks like "(1) dogs; (2) cats; (3) rabbits; and (4) Uzi submachine guns" makes no sense. Third, make sure that your list is grammatically consistent with the sentence which contains it. For an example of how not to construct such a list, consider:

- an item in the present tense;
- was that wrong? (several problems: past tense; doesn't match up with the lead-in ("consider was that wrong"), seems not to flow logically from the previous item on the list, and is in the form of a question);
- consider the context ("consider…consider" makes no sense).

There's no magic formula for formatting a list. Although there are many ways to make a list, I recommend that you stick to two types of lists for now: the itemized list and the nonitemized list. As you become more experienced as a legal writer you might expand your list repertoire, but there's no need at present to make this process more complicated than it needs to be. There are two ways of presenting each type of list, depending on the amount of information each list contains.

i. The Short Itemized List

"Short," of course, is a subjective term. For present purposes, if each part of your itemized list takes up half a line or less of text, it's "short." If one or more parts of the list is longer than half a line, consider it a "long" list and format it accordingly. "Itemized" lists are ones that come to you preformatted with numbers, or ones that require the information to be considered in a particular order. Properly drafted statutes are always itemized, and some recent court opinions have begun to set out tests that should be analyzed in a specific order.

To format a short itemized list within a sentence (which is almost always where it occurs), place a colon after the last word of the sentence before the list, type two spaces, type an opening parenthesis, type "1" (or "a"), type a closing parenthesis, type two spaces, type the text of the first part of the list, type a semicolon, type two spaces, and continue until the list is complete. The list will look like this: (1) each part of the list; (2) should be separated; (3) from each successive part of the list; (4) and the reader should understand implicitly; (5) the organizational principle at work.

ii. The Short Nonitemized List

The short nonitemized list works in almost exactly the same way, but without the numbers. It looks like this. "Lists are: simple; effective; easily read; and helpful to comprehension."

iii. The Long Itemized List

The long itemized list is constructed by placing the number or letter inside parentheses and by positioning it at the first tab stop. The text begins at the next tab stop, and any subsequent lines of text are aligned directly underneath the first line of text but not underneath the number. Text in a long itemized list should be single-spaced, with two line-spaces between the portions of the list. Here's an example:

(a) long itemized lists represent a useful and compact method of taking a large amount of information;

(b) organizing it in a way that's readily understandable and visually appealing for the reader;

(c) and presenting that information in a way that saves space, even though it looks at first as if it takes up a lot of the page.

iv. The Long Nonitemized List

This is the type of list also known as a "bulleted list" because of the use of little black dots to indicate items on the list. Your word processor likely has several different types of bullets available for your use. It's best to use a bullet that is distinctive but not too large. Whichever bullet you choose, it's sensible to create a keyboard shortcut so you can insert it easily in the future.

Here's an example of a long nonitemized list:

- Long nonitemized lists are easy to construct;
- require little in the way of complicated formatting;
- present information to the reader in an appealing format;
- can be particularly helpful when laying out elements of a test;
- and can say in a few words what would otherwise require lengthy exposition.

Although word processing programs allow you to create bulleted lists easily, I caution you against using this option. You're almost always better off making formatting decisions yourself, not accepting what the program presents you with. It can seem to take more time to set up this kind of formatting yourself rather than having the word processing program set it up automatically, but it almost always takes you more time, once you've decided you don't like what the program has done, to reformat the document so that it looks the way you believe it should look.

U. Citations

This one's simple. All your citations should follow the requirements of a citation manual. The two principal manuals taught in law schools are *The ALWD Citation Manual* and *The Bluebook: A Uniform System of Citation*, commonly referred to as "the Bluebook." There are few differences in the approach these two citation manuals take to citing most standard American legal information, although the differences are important and should be observed.

Many states have their own citation manuals, and some law firms, courts, and government offices have their own in-house citation styles. The important thing is to know which citation form is expected of you. In your first year of law school, you will likely be expected to produce citations that conform exactly to ALWD or Bluebook requirements. If you work on a journal in your second and third year of law school, that journal will likely expect proficiency in some standardized citation system. Most law journals use the Bluebook but ALWD is making inroads here. If you're at work, it's likely that you'll be asked to cite sources using either the in-house style, the state citation manual, or the Bluebook. But be careful: lawyers often use the term "Bluebooking" in a generic sense to mean "citing sources," even if the office or jurisdiction doesn't use the actual Bluebook as a citation guide.

V. Widows

In the sense we're using the term here, "widows" refers to text that is severed from the immediately following text by a page break. New paragraphs that begin immediately before a page break are widows, as are headings or subheadings that either have no text or only a line or two of text underneath them.

Your work should not have any widows. So any new paragraph with fewer than three lines of text under it, or any heading with fewer than three lines of the next paragraph under it, should be moved to the top of the next page. You do this by inserting a page break into the text immediately before the widow begins.

Look for widows only at the end of the editing process. If you look for them sooner and then add text before the forced page break, you may find that the text has moved below the naturally occurring page break and that your forced page break now brings you a page of only three or four lines. You can easily fix this, of course—just delete the page break—but you've wasted paper, and you'll have to check for widows again because any change on one page of a document has a ripple effect on all the pages after it. The easiest (and most ecologically friendly) way to check for widows is to preview the electronic version of what the printed document will look like and make your changes before printing the document.

Avoiding widows is important because it makes you look like a professional and that's an important perception to instill in your reader. Avoiding widows is also important because it makes your document easier to read: the reader doesn't have to flip back and forth between pages to figure out what you're saying. And avoiding widows is one more of the many available techniques you should use to help your reader understand your analysis and to persuade your reader of the soundness of your argument.

Creating an appearance of competence in legal writing is like going to court dressed in professional clothes. You all know that the clothes you wear have nothing at all to do with the quality of your legal argument. But between the person making a brilliant legal argument while dressed in jeans and a T-shirt and the person making a sound, though uninspired, argument while dressed in professional clothes, the judge will usually tend to favor the better-dressed argument. This isn't fair, of course. The message's appearance should have nothing to do with its quality: it's supposed to be the quality of the message that counts. But we all live in the real world, and we all know, or should know, that what's fair doesn't always win.

The next part of this manual, then, is the equivalent of a pattern for making a suit. All you have to do is follow the instructions and your legal arguments will walk into court, or your client or instructor's office, looking, if not snazzy, then at least appropriate. They may not prevail—even the best-dressed attorney has to have substance to back up appearance—but they won't lose because of the way they look.

Chapter 7

Common Formatting Elements

The formatting of litigation documents may look complicated at first, but practice quickly makes the process relatively straightforward. And the presence of several common elements that are the same in every document makes the formatting issues even simpler. But before we begin, a quick word on why it's important for young lawyers to know this information.

A. The Lawyer's Role in Document Formatting

A common perception among law students is that they'll all work in firms where secretaries and paralegals will handle such mundane tasks as document formatting, leaving the lawyers to deal with the substantive legal issues. And for some lawyers, this is indeed what happens, at least most of the time. Some, however, will work in offices where there is no support or where there is no help at the moment a document needs to be finalized and filed. And almost all litigation lawyers, at some time in their career, will have to help prepare documents like the ones we'll be discussing here.

But although this likely necessity is a good, practical reason for you to learn how to format documents, you may overlook the two central reasons for learning how to do so. First, no task related to client representation is ever "mundane," and support staff, when you are lucky enough to have them, perform a crucial and difficult job, usually for far less money than you are being paid. Second, you are ultimately responsible for all documents that leave your office under your signature, so when you review documents prepared by yourself or others under your supervision, it is your responsibility to catch and fix all possible problems, including formatting errors, before the document is filed.

Your life in a law firm will be much easier if you remember that everyone—from the most senior name partner to the lowest-paid support person—is a professional whose job is crucial to serving the client's interests in the best way possible. You play an important part in the client's representation, but it is only one part. If you treat the others with whom you work as professionals, you will be treated as a professional yourself. If you don't, you may have a short career in your law firm.

B. Captions

All documents filed with a court should have a caption. You, or your secretary if you're in practice and have one, should set up a caption for each case as soon as the case becomes your responsibility. By doing so, you'll be able to generate identical, accurate captions quickly and easily.

The caption contains all the pertinent information about the litigation and is used by the court to make sure that the document is filed in the correct court file. Different courts have different requirements for captions. The following is a synthesis of some of these rules and contains most of the standard requirements for captions. You should consult the applicable rules in the court where you plan to file the memorandum to augment the suggestions given here.

The first piece of information in the caption is the court's name. This should be preceded by "IN THE" and should be fully capitalized, single-spaced, and centered on the page.

Then comes the plaintiff's name, the word "plaintiff," the designation "v." (not "vs." or "versus"), the docket information for the case, the defendant's name, and the word "defendant." In addition, there are internal marks separating parts of the page. These are usually asterisks, although other symbols—such as colons—are sometimes used.

It's easier to show what a correctly formatted caption looks like than it is to describe it in too much detail:

IN THE CIRCUIT COURT
FOR FICTITIOUS COUNTY

A.B.C. SERVICE, Inc.   *

      Plaintiff   *

v.   *   38-C-981205

GLOBAL OIL COMPANY, et al. *

      Defendants   *

*   *   *   *   *   *   *   *

In this case, there is more than one defendant. Where that happens, the convention is to list only the first defendant itemized on the complaint. The existence of other defendants in this case is shown by "et al." placed after the first defendant's name and by the plural "defendants." Some attorneys will place their client's name on the caption even though that client is not the first-named defendant in the complaint. Although this alternate practice should not affect the document's filing—the clerk's office will likely have the cases filed by docket number and will therefore use that number as a reference—it can lead to confusion and should be avoided. The client's name will be clearly identified in the heading of the document you're filing and that should be sufficient.

Captions for the initial pleadings in a case are formatted slightly differently from the procedure described above. These differences are explained below in the section on initial pleadings.

C. Signature Blocks

Anything a lawyer files with a court requires a signature. The act of signing a court-filed document carries with it more than just an indication of who is filing the paper. Rule 11 of the Federal Rules of Civil Procedure, for example, states:

(a) Signature.

Every pleading, written motion, and other paper shall be signed by at least one attorney of record in the attorney's individual name, or, if the party is not represented by an attorney, shall be signed by the party. Each paper shall state the signer's address and telephone number, if any. Except when otherwise specifically provided by rule or statute, pleadings need not be verified or accompanied by affidavit. An unsigned paper shall be stricken unless omission of the signature is corrected promptly after being called to the attention of attorney or party.

(b) Representations to Court.

By presenting to the court (whether by signing, filing, submitting, or later advocating) a pleading, written motion, or other paper, an attorney or unrepresented party is certifying that to the best of the person's knowledge, information, and belief, formed after an inquiry reasonable under the circumstances,

(1) it is not being presented for any improper purpose, such as to harass or to cause unnecessary delay or needless increase in the cost of litigation;

(2) the claims, defenses, and other legal contentions therein are warranted by existing law or by a non-frivolous argument for the extension, modification, or reversal of existing law or the establishment of new law;

(3) the allegations and other factual contentions have evidentiary support or, if specifically so identified, are likely to have evidentiary support after a reasonable opportunity for further investigation or discovery; and

(4) the denials of factual contentions are warranted on the evidence or, if specifically so identified, are reasonably based on a lack of information or belief.[1]

Failure to comply with this rule can lead to sanctions imposed by the court.

Even though you have a signature block with all the necessary information, if you fail to sign the document in ink many courts will refuse to file it because of the certification requirements of Rule 11 or its state equivalent.

The signature block should contain a line long enough for you to sign your name and any other information the court requires, single-spaced and aligned underneath the beginning of the signature line. Most court rules require your name, the name of your firm, and all relevant contact information, not just the address and telephone number required by Rule 11. Some courts may also require a bar number or other information to show you are entitled to sign and file documents in the court. After double-spacing, you should also indicate which party you represent.

The whole signature block should be preceded by the words "Respectfully submitted" (which themselves should be indented one tab stop) and should be aligned at the tab stop that immediately follows (five tab stops from the left margin). The whole block looks like this:

---

1. Fed. R. Civ. P. 11.

Respectfully submitted,

_____

Polly Peachum
Peachum, McHeath & Lockit, LLP
321 Main Street
Nowhere City, ED 09876
(321) 555-9876 (phone)
(321) 555- 6789 (facsimile)
ppeachum@peachum.com

Attorney for plaintiff/defendant

D. Certificate of Service

Documents filed with courts must show that they have also been sent to the opponents in the case. This is done to prevent the impression that one party is trying to speak to the court without the other side knowing what is going on—an impression referred to as *ex parte* communication. There are some very limited exceptions to this rule—requests for *ex parte* injunctions, for example—but you almost always want to show the court that the other side was sent the document.

The standard means of letting the court know that a document has been served on the other parties to litigation is the certificate of service, formatted as follows:

- the words "certificate of service" are typed bold and are underlined, fully capitalized, and centered on the page;

- after double-spacing and after returning the margin setting to left aligned, type: "I hereby certify that on this (date)—that is, day of (month), (year)—a copy of the foregoing (name of the document) was (method of delivery: mailed, postage prepaid; hand-delivered; sent via Federal Express, and so on) to:

- after double-spacing, list the names and addresses of those who received the document;
- after double-spacing again, include a signature line aligned with the previous signature block and, after single-spacing, include the name of the signer.

Here's an example of a typical certificate of service:

CERTIFICATE OF SERVICE

I hereby certify that on this _____ day of September, 2005, a copy of a Defendant Global Oil Company's Motion for Summary Judgment was mailed, postage prepaid, to:

John A. Smith, Esquire
James B. Smith, Esquire
Smith, Smith & Jones, P.C.
Third Floor
1515 Invented Street
Nowhere City, ED 09876

Jane A. Doe, Esquire
Doe, Ray & Mea, LLP
123 East North Avenue
Nowhere City, ED 09876

_____
Polly Peachum

If the entire certificate of service won't fit on one page, it's best to insert a page break so that it appears on its own page.

Some jurisdictions have very specific requirements for the content of certificates of service. As always, make sure your work conforms to the expectations and requirements of your jurisdiction.

Certificates of service present one trap into which many lawyers fall. The certificate of service must be drafted before the document is sent, yet it represents a lawyer's certification that something *has been* done. But circumstances can change after the certificate has been drafted, especially if it was drafted some time before the service was accomplished. For example, a lawyer may intend to mail a document to opposing counsel but may then arrange a meeting and deliver the document by hand. If the certificate of service reflects that the document was mailed, the certificate is in error.

This example of such an error is not likely to be too disturbing to most courts (although be careful of assuming that something isn't important to a court: treat all deviations from correct practice seriously), but other problems in the certificate—showing an incorrect date of mailing, or showing that a document was sent when, in fact, it was not—will usually be taken very seriously indeed. So, as a general rule, the last thing you should do before serving a document— either by mail or in person—is to check that the certificate of service is correct in all its details. It takes only a few seconds to correct a mistake and it's time well spent.

E. Table of Contents

Tables of contents are usually required only for longer documents like appellate briefs. However, a lengthy memorandum of law filed with a trial court should have a table of contents as well. As a general rule, any memorandum over thirty pages is considered lengthy. Even some complex interoffice memoranda can benefit from tables of contents to orient the reader.

The table of contents is a compilation of the headings and subheadings in your document. These headings are stripped of all special formatting except for capital letters: if the heading was fully capitalized, it remains fully capitalized, and if the heading had initial capital letters these remain capital letters. But the headings are not typed in bold, nor are they underlined, and they are aligned to the left margin, with each level of subheading indented one tab stop in addition to that of the previous level. The page in your text on which each heading appears is shown aligned at the right margin after a tab leader consisting of a series of dots. Your word processor should be able to generate this format without difficulty.

Here's what part of a typical table of contents looks like, using the "headings" examples from the previous chapter. Note that the only heading that is centered is the one for the table itself, and note that this is the only heading that is typed in bold and underlined. Note also that in your table of contents, all headings—not just the headings in your argument section—should be included. So sections like the "question presented" and "statement of facts" are also listed:

<u>TABLE OF CONTENTS</u>

F. Table of Authorities

The table of authorities presents its own challenges. Principal among these is going through the brief and matching the page numbers with each case. Remember that the table of authorities must reflect each page of a brief on which a case reference appears, not just the first page. In other words, every time you use a short form of a citation or the abbreviation "id." to refer to a case, the number of the page on which the citation or id. occurs must be included in your table of authorities.

Your word processor will probably allow you to create tables of authority automatically using an indexing feature. As an alternative, you can go through the brief by hand and note each appearance of a case. This alternative is more time-consuming and is also susceptible to error, but it requires you to read through your brief again, which means you can polish it further and correct errors which you may have overlooked. Also it gives you more control over formatting. No matter which option you choose—automatic or manual—you should always check each page number carefully as one of your last editing steps before filing the brief.

The order of authorities is:

- Cases

- Statutes

- Rules

- Articles

- Other materials

Within each category, organize the material alphabetically or numerically. Thus, in the "Cases" category, a case with the first name "*Andre*" comes before "*Zachary*," even though *Andre* might be a trial court opinion and *Zachary* comes from the Supreme Court. In the "Statutes" category, constitutions come first (federal before state), then federal statutes and state statutes. If you cite from the statutory provisions of more than one state, organize the states alphabetically. Within statutory schemes, organize the material numerically (18 U.S.C. comes before 28 U.S.C., and so on). The same order applies to the "Rules" section. "Articles" are organized alphabetically by name of the principal author. "Other materials" are organized as logically as possible, alphabetically if possible, then chronologically, then numerically.

Within the "Cases" category, cases should appear in full-citation format, with the following exceptions:

- Cases should only show the first page on which the case appears in the reporter. If the citation in the analysis reflects a pinpoint page reference, this should be removed when the citation is reproduced in the table of contents.

- The case should have no subsequent history in the table of contents, even though proper citation practice might require that history when the case appears in the analysis section of the brief.

- If the citation system you are using requires you to parallel cite a case, the parallel citation should appear in the table of contents. And if the case has not yet been published but appears in an electronic database, you should follow the citation manual's rules for citing the case in the table of contents.

You should include all cases in the table of authorities, even cases that appear to have little consequence to the analysis. For example, if you include, in a parenthetical reference, the fact that one case quotes from, or cites, a previous case, both cases should be reflected in the table of contents. In other words, the table should be complete and not list merely the cases you believe to be most important.

If a reference to a case, statute, or rule appears on almost every page of your brief, you can substitute the word "passim" for page references. As a general rule, the reference should appear on more than ten pages of your brief before you use this shorthand.

Split each case citation onto two lines: the name of the case on the first line and the locating information (volume number, volume, first page number, and so on) on the second line, followed by a dotted tab leader aligned with the right margin and the page numbers on which the case appears, separated by commas and a space. This same principle applies to law review articles, where the break will typically come in the middle of the article's title.

Here's an example of a typical table of authorities. Please refer to it only for formatting purposes and not as a guide for citation formatting:

TABLE OF AUTHORITIES

CASES

STATUTES

LAW REVIEW ARTICLES

Chapter 8

Litigation Documents

This chapter follows the standard progress of civil litigation, from prefiling analysis and predictive documents, through the filing of the initial pleadings, the discovery process, trial, and finally appeal. The order is not exact of course: many cases will interpose motions to dismiss between complaints and answers, and the order and nature of discovery is different in almost every case. In fact, it is almost impossible to generalize about litigation except to say, unhelpfully, that every case will be different. Nonetheless, the types of documents described in this chapter are those you will likely be asked to draft as law students or junior lawyers.

A. Interoffice Memoranda

The first legal document you'll likely be asked to draft—either as a law student or once you're a practicing lawyer—is an interoffice memorandum. This document is the standard vehicle for recording analysis and transmitting information within a law office. Memoranda are placed in various subfiles of a principal file and will often be referred to, and relied upon, months or even years after they've been written. Also they'll often go into a firm's research file so that subsequent researchers will have a starting place to begin their own research.

Interoffice memoranda are usually not sent to a firm's clients, and this can lead junior lawyers to be less concerned with the formality of these documents. After all, only the other lawyers in the firm will see them, probably not the clients. But this is a dangerous approach to take. For a junior lawyer, who may have little or no contact with the firm's clients, the senior lawyers reviewing internal memoranda are the clients whom that lawyer must serve. If you take this approach, and treat your senior lawyers as your clients, your work will be carefully prepared and presented and they'll quickly learn to trust you. That trust is an important step in moving forward within the law firm. So while you should always write memoranda reflecting careful and thoughtful legal reasoning, you should—for your own sake—present that reasoning in a careful, professional manner.

The word "memorandum" has two very different meanings in the law. Here we're considering the interoffice memorandum. Later, we'll consider formatting issues relating to memoranda filed with courts. Interoffice memoranda are internal documents and tend to be predictive in style. By contrast, trial memoranda are filed with courts and are therefore, with a few very limited exceptions, public documents, and they are usually written in a persuasive style.

i.   Initial Formatting

Traditionally, the first word in every memorandum is "memorandum." It's usually placed in the center of the page and is typed bold-faced and in all capital letters. Very cautious lawyers who want to be sure that all work done on behalf of a client is demonstrably privileged may first want to place a header on every page of the memorandum, indicating that the contents are confidential and subject to the attorney-client privilege. If you do this, make sure that the header is typed in a smaller font size than that of the regular text.

After typing "**MEMORANDUM**," double-space, type a solid line across the page, then double-space again. Your word processor may automatically reformat the line, making it bolder and thicker than it appeared when you typed it. This is one automatic reformatting you can allow.

In capital letters, but not bold-faced, you should next type the word "TO," followed by a colon and two tab stops, then the name of the memo's recipient. Then reset your line spacing for single-spacing and on successive lines type the words "FROM" (followed by a colon, one tab stop, and your name), "DATE" (followed by a colon, two tab stops, and the date) and the abbreviation "RE" (followed by a colon, two tab stops, and the subject of the memorandum).

Finally, reset the line spacing for double-spacing and again type a solid line across the page. The following should be the result, with the optional header:

CONFIDENTIAL: ATTORNEY-CLIENT PRIVILEGED

MEMORANDUM

TO: George McHeath
FROM: Polly Peachum
DATE: John Doe Deposition
RE: July 10, 2005

Memoranda typically aren't signed, nor is there a place for a special signature block. In order to show that a memorandum is in final form and is ready to be delivered to its recipient, the writer will usually initial it beside the writer's name.

ii. Other Formatting Issues

Section headings for research memoranda typically follow the format: "question presented," "short answer," "statement of facts," "analysis," and "conclusion." These headings should be capitalized, bold-faced, underlined, and centered on the page. In practice, you may sometimes omit the "statement of facts," but it's usually helpful for your reader to know the factual basis for your analysis. Your analysis could be flawed if your understanding of the facts is wrong or incomplete, and it's helpful for your reader—who might have a better appreciation of the facts than you—to know this.

When you work in a law firm, you may find yourself drafting memoranda in a looser format, and you will have to draft different section headings according to the needs of the specific document you're drafting. Subheadings should follow the formatting rules contained in the previous chapter on formatting issues, as should other formatting elements such as page numbers, block quotes, and term definitions.

B. Initial Pleadings

The complaint and the answer are the two principal pleadings in civil litigation. All other documents filed with the court during the course of the litigation are known as "motions" or "papers." The form for pleadings can differ from jurisdiction to jurisdiction. The formats contained below are generic and, as with all other formatting suggestions in this manual, should be revised to conform to local rules or practice.

i. Complaints

The complaint is the document that initiates litigation. You will usually be required to file additional documents with the complaint: a summons and a cover sheet giving the court some basic information about the case, for example. You might also be asked to disclose all corporate interests at stake so the court can assign the case to a judge with no financial interest in the outcome.

Almost all courts require complaints to be accompanied by a filing fee. You should check with your jurisdiction for the correct amount of this fee and the acceptable means of paying the fee. Unless you are filing complaints in this particular jurisdiction on a regular basis, it is good practice to check with the clerk's office each time you intend to file a complaint: filing fees have a tendency to go up, and failure to have the correct fee will usually prompt the clerk to refuse to file the complaint.

a. Caption

The caption for a complaint is similar, but not identical, to the captions you'll create for motions and other papers to be filed with the court. A complaint's caption has all the information, and the same appearance, as those other captions, but with two differences. First, since this is the first document filed and no docket number has yet been assigned to the litigation, the space for the docket number should be indicated but left blank. Second, the complaint should list each party involved in the litigation, not just the first-named party on each side, and it should have the address of each party typed directly under that party's role in the litigation (as well as the name and address of the party's resident agent if the party is a corporation). As a result, the process server will have the necessary information to serve the complaint and the defendants will have the necessary information to serve any responsive pleadings.

An example is found on the next page.

b. Parties

It's a good idea to have a separate section at the beginning of your complaint headed "the parties," in which you briefly introduce all plaintiffs (in a separate paragraph for each) and what you know about all defendants (again, in separate paragraphs for each). This is particularly useful if you're planning to bring the action in federal court and need to establish diversity of citizenship, or if you're

IN THE CIRCUIT COURT
FOR FICTITIOUS COUNTY

A.B.C. SERVICE, Inc.   *

     Plaintiff   *

     987 North Avenue   *
     Nowhere City
     ED 09876   *

v.   *   Docket No: _____

GLOBAL OIL COMPANY   *

     Defendant   *

     Peter Grimes   *
     Resident Agent
                                  *

     654 South Avenue
     Nowhere City   *
     ED 09876

                                  *

WELL DESIGNED AND
MANUFACTURED WIDGET   *
COMPANY

                                  *

     Defendant
                                  *

     Donald Giovanni
     Resident Agent   *

     321 East Avenue   *
     Nowhere City
     ED 09876   *

                                  *

*   *   *   *   *   *   *   *   *

trying to keep the case from being removed to federal court and are trying to show there's no diversity.

c. Jurisdiction and Venue

Federal courts in particular like to know that they have jurisdiction, so you should include a separate section headed "jurisdiction and venue," with some paragraphs showing that the case meets the jurisdictional and venue requirements for bringing the complaint in the court in which it's been brought. Although this practice is especially important in federal complaints, it's a good idea to follow it in all complaints.

d. Allegations

Some complaints are so confusing that one suspects they were drafted by plaintiffs intentionally to confuse anyone who reads them. This is not good practice. You can be sure that the defense will try to turn any lack of clarity to its own benefit and that the judge will likely be unhappy with any complaint that's too hard to read.

Often the relevant rule of procedure will require you to structure your complaint so that each allegation is contained within its own numbered paragraph. Even if the controlling rules in the jurisdiction where you'll be filing the complaint don't require this, it's still a good practice to follow: putting each new thought in a new paragraph forces you to put down the contested issues in as logical a sequence as possible.

It's best to structure your complaint using subheadings, just as you would in a brief filed with the court. So have a section for "factual allegations" under which you put all the factual allegations necessary to make a prima facie case. Remember that one of the purposes of the complaint is to present a set of allegations that are sufficient to state a viable cause of action in your jurisdiction. If you omit a necessary factual predicate, your complaint is open to a motion to dismiss for failure to state a claim.

It's particularly important to structure your factual allegations in short paragraphs that are noncontroversial and straightforward, because you want to encourage the defendant to admit as many of these allegations as possible. An allegation that's admitted in the answer need not be litigated—it's established as fact—so you want the defendant to admit as much as possible. If you put three factual allegations into one paragraph, two of which are uncontested and one of which is very much contested, the defendant may deny all the factual allegations in the single paragraph. But if you place each factual allegation into a separate paragraph, the defendant will likely admit the two uncontested allegations and deny only the contested one.

e. Counts

Once you've made all the factual allegations you're going to make, it's time to get to the "counts" of the complaint. These are the legal heart of the complaint. First, however, you should reincorporate all your facts at the start of each count in the complaint.

This is a simple process. Assume that your factual allegations are finished at paragraph 55. On the next line, you should type "Count One," bold-faced, centered, and in all capital letters. Then, after a single space, type the name of the particular cause of action you will assert, again bold-faced, centered, in all capital letters, but this time contained within parentheses. Then double-space, align your cursor at the left hand margin, tab one stop, and in normal print type the next number in the paragraph sequence followed by a period ("56." in this case). Then tab over one more stop and type "Plaintiff incorporates by reference the allegations in Paragraphs one through fifty-five above, as though fully set forth herein in full." The actual allegations necessary to establish the cause of action start in the next paragraph.

An example should make this process clearer:

COUNT 1
(STRICT LIABILITY)

56. Plaintiff incorporates by reference the allegations in Paragraphs one through fifty-five above, as though fully set forth herein in full.
57. …

f. Ad Damnum Clause

In the *Ad Damnum* clause you tell the court, and the other side, what your client wants for the civil wrong you allege the other side has committed. This is a clause where practice can differ from jurisdiction to jurisdiction. In some states, for example, you may be required to itemize the damages your client seeks in each count of the complaint, while other states may be satisfied with one *ad damnum* clause at the end. Moreover, some states require a specific dollar amount in the *ad damnum* clause, while others do not.

If your jurisdiction requires a specific dollar amount, you should be careful to know what the implications of this requirement are. For example, if the jury comes back with a recovery in excess of the amount you sought in the complaint, are you capped at the amount you requested? If so, you should be sure to ask for an amount at the outer limits of what you think you'll be able to prove. Just in case, you should be familiar with the rules allowing you to amend your complaint after a jury verdict.

This can be particularly significant if the case can be removed to federal court, something defendants will try to do if the complaint gives them grounds for removal and if they believe there's an advantage to them to be gained in federal courts. When the complaint doesn't provide a specific amount of damages, the defendant has several more hoops to jump through in order to remove the case than if the complaint seeks an exact dollar amount in excess of the relevant jurisdictional amount.

Here's one way to draft an *ad damnum* clause at the end of a complaint, giving a specific dollar amount. Be very careful to check the civil procedure rules in the jurisdiction in which your complaint will be filed before following this example too closely.

After the last numbered paragraph setting out the legal predicate for the last cause of action you're asserting, double-space, tab over one stop, and, in all capital letters, type "wherefore," followed by a comma. Then type, in lower-case, "plaintiff demands judgment from defendant in the amount of $x,000,000.00, together with interest, the costs of this action and attorney's fees, and any further relief this Court deems just and proper." If you're seeking any additional relief, this is the place to ask for it. If you don't ask for additional relief, you might not be able to get it: the complaint typically defines the boundaries of the relief your client is seeking.

g. Signature Block

After you've finished your itemized counts, you should type, "Respectfully submitted," and insert a signature block. There is no need for a certificate of service in a complaint because you will have a return of service from the process server showing that the complaint was served, once you decide to have the complaint served on the defendants. Moreover, you can't indicate that you've served the documents on the defendants' lawyers because you don't yet know who those lawyers will be.

h. Demand for Jury Trial

In many jurisdictions the plaintiff must demand a jury trial when the complaint is filed. This demand is usually made by the drafting of a simple document, although in some jurisdictions the jury trial demand is merely added to the complaint as its last section. If a separate document is required, it should have the same caption as the complaint, a centered heading with "demand for jury trial" in capital letters, bold-faced and underlined, and then, indented but aligned at the left margin and in normal text, the following: "Plaintiff [insert plaintiff's name] hereby demands a trial by jury for all issues triable by a jury." Then you should type, "Respectfully submitted," and insert a signature block, exactly as you did in the complaint.

Remember that if you're seeking exclusively equitable relief, you won't be able to get a jury trial and that there are some statutory causes of action that specify bench trials instead of jury trials. Be sure to check that you have pled issues that entitle you to a jury trial before asking for one. The defense will relish the opportunity to make you look incompetent before the judge when it moves to quash your jury demand if you're not entitled to a jury trial.

ii. Answers

The answer should be a mirror image of the complaint, with each paragraph in the answer responding precisely to the allegations in the same numbered paragraph in the complaint. This pattern only changes at the end, when the answer lists the defendant's affirmative answers.

Some jurisdictions permit you to file what are known as "general denial" answers. In those jurisdictions, an answer usually takes up one page and consists principally of a statement to the effect that "Defendant [insert the defendant's name] generally denies all allegations as pled in Plaintiff's complaint."

If this is a sufficient answer in your jurisdiction, you should always follow this form rather than giving the plaintiff more information in the form of an itemized answer. A general denial answer is substantially less expensive for your client and can be particularly beneficial to you if you're planning to remove the case to federal court. Although federal courts require itemized answers,[1] if a complaint has been appropriately answered according to state court re-

---

1. Fed. R. Civ. P. 8(b).

quirements before removal, that answer should be deemed sufficient for federal court purposes as well.

a. Responses

If you're preparing an itemized answer, there are several appropriate responses to the allegations in a complaint. If you have no objection to a paragraph's allegations, you should write, "Defendant admits the allegations in paragraph x." If you disagree with the allegations, you should write, "Defendant denies the allegations in paragraph x." If the complaint is poorly drafted and contains multiple allegations in a paragraph, one of which you admit while seeking to deny the others, you should write, "Defendant admits the allegation in paragraph x that [insert the admitted allegation]. Defendant denies all other allegations in paragraph x."

If you don't know the answer, because the plaintiff has made an allegation that will require discovery, write, "Defendant is without the knowledge or information necessary to admit or deny the allegations in paragraph x." That should be treated by the court as a denial, although a more honest one than a straight-out denial of the allegations. Be sure that this is the case in your jurisdiction before filing the answer. If it isn't, or if you aren't sure, you should add a second sentence: "Accordingly, defendant denies the allegations as pled in paragraph x."

In some cases, a plaintiff will include a statement of law in the complaint. The defendant is typically only required to answer factual allegations, so the appropriate response in this situation is as follows: "The allegations in paragraph x contain conclusions of law for which no answer is necessary." Be absolutely sure that the allegations in the paragraph truly are ones of law before making this answer.

When you encounter a paragraph where the plaintiff has incorporated, by reference, all the allegations of the previous paragraphs, the appropriate response is as follows: "Defendant incorporates by reference the responses in Paragraphs one through x above, as though fully set forth herein in full." That way, the answer mirrors the complaint in every detail and the court can tell with relative ease what's been admitted and what's been denied.

b. Affirmative Defenses

The defendant's work isn't done after all the complaint's allegations are answered because now the defendant must assert whatever affirmative defenses are appropriate. There are many such defenses and now's the time to go on record with them. Remember, though, that in federal court at least, you'll be expected to have support for these affirmative defenses and you'll be opening your client up to discovery and initial disclosure on those affirmative defenses you assert.[2]

This marks a change in practice from the times when defendants would include a laundry list of affirmative defenses, some of them with—at best—a tenuous connection to the allegations in the complaint. This may still be the practice in some jurisdictions. If you work at a firm that usually practices in state court but is now filing answers in federal court, or vice versa, you should make sure that all attorneys working on the file review the relevant rules of civil procedure to make sure everyone understands the implications of those rules on your drafting practices. And if you are filing in an out-of-state jurisdiction, you should have a local counsel in that jurisdiction check your pleading to make sure it conforms with local rules and practice.

Affirmative defenses are easy to format. For each, center the heading and in bold, capitalized, and underlined letters, type, "[first, second, third, and so on] affirmative defense." Then double space, align the cursor at the left margin, indent the first line, and type a brief description of the affirmative defense you are asserting. If you claim,

---

2. Fed. R. Civ. P. 26.

for example, that the complaint is time-barred, type, "Plaintiff's complaint is barred by the applicable statute of limitations."

At the end of the entire document, type, "Respectfully submitted," and insert a signature block, just as in the complaint. The answer should have a certificate of service because you know who the plaintiff's lawyers are.

C. Discovery Documents

Once the litigation is underway, you will likely shift into the discovery phase. Discovery documents pose few formatting challenges. Although these days they are usually not filed with the court unless there is a dispute over the requested discovery, they should nonetheless be drafted in proper form so they can be filed if necessary.

i. Interrogatories

These written questions to the opposing side are often the first salvo in the discovery battle. They should be used to learn basic information about the other side's case and should be drafted as carefully as possible to minimize objections and refusals to answer from your opponent.

a. Caption

Interrogatories should carry the basic caption for the litigation. In addition, the title of the document should indicate the name of the person to whom the interrogatories are directed or that they are intended for a corporate designee if you don't know the name of that person.

b. Definitions and Instructions

Before you ask your questions, you should define the more common terms you plan to use in the interrogatories. For example, if you have a corporate defendant and you will be using that defendant's name frequently in the interrogatories, you may prefer to use a shortened form of the name. This is accomplished by stating the name you intend to use and indicating what that name means. For example: "The name 'Global' shall mean defendant Global Oil Company." This method of defining a term differs from that used in other legal documents discussed in the chapter "General Formatting Issues."

You should also include any instructions you want the respondent to follow. You should, for example, instruct the respondent of the continuing nature of the questions you are asking and of the respondent's obligation to supplement the answers later if additional information comes to light. Lawyers will already know of this obligation, but it is good practice to specify all such instructions in the discovery document in case of a later dispute.

Each definition and instruction should have its own paragraph, and each paragraph should be indicated by a letter, not a number. The interrogatories themselves will be numbered and it would be confusing to have two sets of numbered paragraphs within the same document.

c. Questions

Each interrogatory should be as short as possible and should seek specific information. Although the limits placed on the number of interrogatories by many jurisdictions make it tempting to try to get as much information as possible from each question, a loosely drafted interrogatory will often receive a blanket objection and refusal to answer because the question is impossible to understand or is unduly burdensome. If this happens, the interrogatory has been wasted unless you are successful in persuading the court to compel the other side to answer.

If you are limited in the number of interrogatories you can ask, it is often good practice to ask fewer than the maximum number allowed during the first round of discovery. That way, you have some questions left in reserve should something come up later in the litigation that requires information or clarification. And remember that most jurisdictions will count subparts of a larger question as separate questions for purposes of the limit: if you're limited to, for example, 25 interrogatories, you can't evade the limit by asking 20 questions but with each question having 50 subparts.

Each question should take up one numbered paragraph. If you ask any subpart questions, these should be separately indicated and each labeled by a letter.

Some attorneys will leave a space after each question as if to leave room for the person answering the question to write in the answer. This is an old-fashioned style and is no longer necessary, unless required by rule in your jurisdiction or by the attorney for whom you're working.

d. Certificate of Service

Even though discovery documents aren't usually filed with the court, you should include a standard certificate of service with each set of discovery requests, showing when each set was delivered and how it was delivered. Although some lawyers may send out interrogatories and document requests at the same time and have only one certificate of service to cover both, this is not a good practice. It's better to certify each set of documents separately so that if a dispute arises, you need only file the specific set of documents in dispute with the court.

e. Responses

When responding to discovery requests, you should respond in the same order as the requests were made. In other words, if you have objections to the definitions and instructions supplied in the request, you should outline each objection in the same order as the definition or instruction appeared, and then you should go through the requests in order.

Before indicating your response to the discovery request, you should first repeat the request to which you are responding. That can involve a lot of typing, so you should set that stage in process as soon as you receive the discovery requests. Creating an early shell document, in which all the discovery requests are typed out in full and there are spaces in which to fit the responses when you've checked them with your client, will save you from rushing to get the responses ready for filing within the designated time.

Although each request was originally filed with simply a number designating the different paragraphs, the response should give separate subheadings—"Interrogatory 1," "Response to Interrogatory 1," and so on. This practice is necessary to prevent the reader from being confused as to when the request ends and the response begins.

Even though most legal documents are double-spaced, the requests to which you are responding can be single-spaced. Even though each request and response will have its own heading, the single spacing provides another helpful visual cue to the reader marking the boundaries between requests and responses.

For each response, you should first indicate if you are objecting—usually with a one word sentence to that effect: "Objection." You should then specify the ground for each objection, citing the rule on which you base your objection: the federal rules require specific grounds for objections[3] and your jurisdiction likely will as well. If you cannot, or will not, answer the request, you should then indicate that. If, however, you plan to respond to the request, you should precede that response by indicating that it is given without waiving your objection. In this way your objection is preserved for later ruling by the court if necessary.

---

3. Fed. R. Civ. P. 33(b)(4).

f. Signing

The federal rules require that all interrogatory responses be answered "separately and fully in writing under oath."[4] Moreover, the answers "are to be signed by the person making them, and the objections signed by the attorney making them."[5] It is likely that your jurisdiction will have a similar requirement. This means that in addition to the regular signature block, modified to certify that your signature relates to the objections made in the responses, you must also prepare an affidavit or declaration on behalf of the client or client's representative who is actually answering the questions. A form for affidavits is included below in the section on documents that commonly accompany trial memoranda.

ii. Document Requests

Document requests follow the same format as interrogatories. Typically, you should reproduce the definitions and instructions for interrogatories in your document requests, except those that are only interrogatory-specific.

You should also include in your definitions the term "document." In defining the term you should be as broad as possible, because you don't want to give your opponent the chance to withhold a crucial document because it doesn't fall within your definition. If your jurisdiction has a set of definitions of a "document," you should incorporate that into your definition. But if the jurisdiction's definition isn't broad enough for your purposes, you shouldn't limit yourself to it unless jurisdiction rules prevent you from being broader.

Within your definition of "document," you should include handwritten, typed, computer-generated, or otherwise produced tangible matter (hard copies) and any nontangible matter (electronic

---

4. Fed. R. Civ. P. 33(b)(1).
5. Fed. R. Civ. P. 33(b)(2).

copies), as well as drafts (showing the development of a document), and all nonidentical copies. These nonidentical copies can often be very valuable, especially if they contain notes written by people involved in the litigation. You can give examples of what the term "document" means (drafts, memoranda, correspondence, telex messages, fax transmissions, envelopes, notes, e-mails, and so on), but you should indicate that the list is not exclusive and that you are including writings of every kind within your definition.

Your instructions to your opponent should include where and when you expect the documents to be delivered and in what form. You would usually want your documents to be produced at your office, so you should give that address in the instructions, even though your office address is also on the signature block at the end of the discovery request. If you want the documents to be delivered somewhere else, you should give that address in the instructions. And if you will accept the documents in some electronic format—a format becoming increasingly more common with the prevalence of high-volume scanners—you should indicate that in the instructions as well.

When asking for documents, you should always remember to ask for all documents referred to by the other side in its pleadings and in its responses to your interrogatories. You should also ask for all documents shown to any experts the other side intends to call to testify and any documents those experts have forwarded to the opposing attorneys.

iii. Requests for Admission

While interrogatories and document requests usually come at the beginning of the discovery process, requests for admissions often come much later, often shortly before trial. Requests for admission are usually used to minimize the administrative burden of having to prove facts that are not really in dispute, or that certain documents are genuine and therefore their genuineness need not be established at trial. Because any fact admitted to under this process will usually be deemed to have been conclusively established,[6] you should avoid wasting these requests on things you know the other side cannot or will not admit as true.

Requests for admissions, and the responses to them, follow the same format as that for other discovery documents.

D. Memoranda of Law

Memoranda of law are the principal means a lawyer uses to deliver legal and factual information to a trial court. Although the memorandum of law shares part of its name with the interoffice memorandum, it is a very different document: it is written in a persuasive style in order to obtain a result from a court, and it has a very different appearance.

In formatting terms, though, the document should be relatively simple for you to prepare since it's assembled from elements you've already drafted for other documents. A memorandum of law has a standard caption, tables of contents, and authorities if long enough, and it concludes with a signature block and certificate of service. Internally, the document should follow the formatting suggestions explained in the chapter on general formatting issues.

E. Documents Accompanying the Memorandum of Law

It's rare that a memorandum of law is filed on its own. More typically, memoranda are accompanied by the motions they support, and often they are filed with proposed orders. If the memorandum

---

6. Fed. R. Civ. P. 36(b).

contains some assertions of fact, it will likely be accompanied by an affidavit or declaration.

Although these documents are short and present few formatting challenges, they can be easily overlooked until the memorandum is finished and ready to be filed. Rather than draft them at the last second, or even worse, forgetting to draft them at all and having to ask the court for permission to add them later, it's better to draft all accompanying documents first and have them on file ready to include with the memorandum when it's completed.

Although not described separately in this chapter, all these documents should be accompanied by a letter to the clerk when sent for filing. If your jurisdiction requires you to file additional copies of documents, the letter should indicate how many copies of the documents you are filing, along with the original. If you would like a date-stamped copy of the documents for your records, something many lawyers want in their files as evidence that a document was filed with the clerk's office on a particular day, your letter should indicate that as well. So be sure to file enough copies with the original memorandum so the clerk can stamp one and return it to you. Even if you ask for a date-stamped copy, the clerk will not provide one unless you have enough copies to meet the court's filing requirements and an additional one to be returned to you.

i. Motions

Motions are the formal documents that ask the court to do something. The memorandum in support of the motion is the document that gives the court the reasons you think it should act or not act. But without the motion, the memorandum is just a group of reasons without a request.

Only the moving party need file a motion. Unless the rule in your jurisdiction is different, the party opposing the motion need not file its own motion to the effect that it is opposing: a memorandum in opposition to the motion is sufficient. If, on the other hand, you are filing a cross-motion along with your opposition, that would require a separate motion.

a. Caption

A motion should have the identical caption as the memorandum in support of it. The only difference is that the heading should indicate that this is the motion, not the memorandum in support of the motion.

There are only a few standard headings for motions. These motions, such as motions to dismiss, motions for summary judgment, motions in limine (in civil cases), and motions to suppress evidence (in criminal cases), all require little additional clarification. But you can file a motion asking a court to do anything within its authority, and a trial court has very broad authority. There is no formula for creating these motion headings except that, as a general rule, the heading should state with as much particularity as possible what you want the court to do and it should be as short as possible.

b. Substance of the Motion

The motion should identify the party who is making the motion and the attorneys who are filing it, and it should indicate the relief that's sought, along with a very general statement of the legal authority for that relief. Often that legal authority will come in the form of a rule of civil procedure or evidence or a Constitutional provision. Wherever it comes from, you should provide some authority that allows the court to act in the way you're requesting.

Then, in separately numbered paragraphs, the motion should identify the specific legal principle that allows the court to act (with the language often taken directly from the rule that supplies the authority for your motion); should indicate that the memorandum in support contains the reasons for the desired relief; and should specifically incorporate the contents of the memorandum into the motion.

Finally, the motion should have a concluding paragraph that begins with the capitalized word "WHEREFORE" and contains the request for relief from the court. That request should include both the positive and the negative implications of the desired relief. For example, if you're asking the court for summary judgment, you should ask the court to enter judgment in your client's favor and against the other side. Leave no doubt as to what will happen if the court grants your request.

The motion should conclude with a signature block identical to that contained in the memorandum in support. And it should contain a duplicate certificate of service, identical to that attached to the memorandum in support except for this document's different name. Although one certificate of service could cover all relevant documents—motion, memorandum in support, and proposed order (if any)—it's better form to have a separate certificate for the motion and the memorandum in case there's any question that the opposing party received both documents.

Here's an example of a motion. As always, it represents a generic document that should be tailored to meet the specific requirements of your jurisdiction:

IN THE CIRCUIT COURT
FOR FICTITIOUS COUNTY

A.B.C. SERVICE, Inc.	*	
Plaintiff	*	
v.	*	38-C-981205
GLOBAL OIL COMPANY, et al.	*	
Defendant	*	

*   *   *   *   *   *   *   *   *

DEFENDANT GLOBAL OIL COMPANY'S
<u>MOTION FOR SUMMARY JUDGMENT</u>

Defendant Global Oil Company, by and through its attorneys Polly Peachum and Peachum, McHeath & Lockit, LLP, hereby move for summary judgment pursuant to Fictitious State Rule of Civil Procedure 56. The grounds for this motion are:

1. There is no genuine dispute as to any material fact, and defendant Global Oil Company is entitled to judgment as a matter of law.

2. Additional grounds for this motion are set forth in the accompanying Memorandum, which is incorporated herein.

WHEREFORE, defendant Global Oil Company requests that this Court enter judgment in its favor and against plaintiff A.B.C. Service, Inc.

Respectfully submitted,

_____

Polly Peachum
Peachum, McHeath & Lockit, LLP
(321) 555-9876 (phone)
(321) 555-6789 (facsimile)
ppeachum@peachum.com

Attorney for defendant
Global Oil Company

CERTIFICATE OF SERVICE

I hereby certify that on this _____ day of September, 2005, a copy of Defendant Global Oil Company's Motion for Summary Judgment was mailed, postage prepaid, to:

John A. Smith, Esquire
James B. Smith, Esquire
Smith, Smith & Jones, P.C.
Third Floor
1515 Invented Street
Nowhere City, ED 09876

Jane A. Doe, Esquire
Doe, Ray & Mea, LLP
123 East North Avenue
Nowhere City, ED 09876

_____

Polly Peachum

ii. Proposed Orders

Judges often, but by no means always, ask the parties to file proposed orders that represent the relief they're seeking. The judge isn't asking you to write an opinion—that's something the judge, or the judge's law clerk, will write. But sometimes the judge doesn't need to write a formal opinion and will just enter an order, the formal document that records the judge's decision concerning a motion. If the judge asks for proposed orders, both sides should submit them so the judge can choose the order that reflects the decision the judge wants to take.

Don't worry about trying to read the judge's mind when you draft the proposed order. If the judge wants to modify the relief you're seeking or wants to add something to the order you've submitted, the judge can handwrite—or interlineate, in the fancy language courts sometimes use—any changes. Your proposed order should stick as closely as possible to the relief you're seeking in the motion. But no document you will draft is more individual than a proposed order. Each judge has a different way of writing an order and you should scour your files to see if you have any previous orders from the judge so you can tailor the document as closely as possible to that judge's individual style.

a. Caption

The caption is exactly the same as the caption for the motion and the memorandum in support of it, with the capitalized word "ORDER" as the document's title.

b. Substance of the Order

The order should note that the court has considered filings from both parties. If you're opposing a motion, you will know the names of both motions and can use those. But if you're filing the motion, you won't know what the other side will call its opposition. In that case, it's safer to indicate that the court has considered your motion and any opposition filed in response to it. You should also indicate that the court will write a written opinion that is dated the same day as the order. The judge can cross this sentence out if no opinion will accompany the order.

Then comes the heart of the order. Because the judge is mandating a result, the words indicating the judge's decision are often capitalized. And because it's important that the date of the judge's decision be known, you should include a space for the date in the body of the order rather than leaving room for it at the end. Then, in numbered paragraphs, spell out everything you want the judge to do. This means not only that the judge should grant your motion but also that any relief flowing from that decision is also granted. And since you want everyone to get copies of the decision, you should include an instruction to the clerk of the court to send those copies to counsel for the parties. Finally, of course, you should leave room for the judge's signature, name, and jurisdiction. If you don't know the identity of the judge, include the signature line only with the name of the court but, of course, without the judge's name.

On the page oppsite is a generic example of a proposed order granting a motion. The flowery language is appropriate for some judges and not for others.

iii. Affidavits and Declarations

Even though these documents are usually signed by clients, or others who are saying something on the client's behalf, they are prepared by attorneys. You should check each jurisdiction's rules about affidavits and declarations to see if there are specific requirements you must follow or information that must be contained in them. As always, the suggestions here are for generic, and not jurisdiction-specific, documents.

The only difference between affidavits and declarations is the method by which the information in them is warranted to be accu-

IN THE CIRCUIT COURT
FOR FICTITIOUS COUNTY

A.B.C. SERVICE, Inc.   *

    Plaintiff   *

v.   *   38-C-981205

GLOBAL OIL COMPANY, et al. *

    Defendant   *

*   *   *   *   *   *   *   *   *

ORDER

Upon consideration of defendant Global Oil Company's Motion for Summary Judgment and any opposition filed thereto, and for the reasons stated in a Memorandum Opinion of even date, IT IS, this _____ day of _____, 2005, by the Court ORDERED:

1. That defendant's Motion BE, and the same hereby IS, GRANTED;

2. That judgment BE, and the same hereby IS, ENTERED in defendant's favor and against plaintiff.

3. That the Clerk of the Court mail a copy of this Order and accompanying Memorandum Opinion to counsel of record for all parties.

Judge Diana Trapes
Circuit Court for Fictitious County

rate. An affidavit is a document that is taken to a notary public who certifies the affiant's oath, signs the document, and usually attaches a seal. A declaration is a self-warranting document.

An affidavit and a declaration each starts with a regular caption and a heading indicating which type of document it is and giving the name of the affiant or declarer. The first paragraph then sets out the supporting information necessary for someone to testify. Usually this will involve the assertion that the affiant or declarer is over eighteen years of age, has personal knowledge of the information in the document, and is competent to testify as a witness.

Each subsequent piece of information should be in a separate, numbered paragraph. If the affidavit or declaration is in support of a summary judgment motion and the affiant or declarer is an expert witness, you should list the person's credentials to be an expert and before the substantive information begins, you should include a paragraph noting that the opinions expressed are done so to the appropriate evidentiary standard (reasonable degree of scientific certainty, or whatever is appropriate under the circumstances).

a. Affidavits

Affidavits and declarations only differ substantially at the end. Both documents require affirmatory language, place and date information, and a signature. In an affidavit, you should also include space for the notary to sign and seal the document.

Here's an example of affirmatory language for both the affiant and the notary. It's important to leave space to indicate the date of expiration of the notary's commission. And as always, beware of jurisdictional differences that may exist where you're filing this document:

I SOLEMNLY AFFIRM under the penalties of perjury and upon personal knowledge that the contents of the aforegoing paper are true and correct.

_____

William Budd

STATE OF _____

CITY/COUNTY OF _____

On this _____ day of _____, 2005, William Budd appeared before me, was known to me or provided evidence of identity, took an oath in due form of law and executed the aforegoing Affidavit, as indicted by my signature and seal below.

_____

Notary Public

My commission expires:

Sometimes you must mail the affidavit to a witness and ask the witness to execute it in front of a notary and send it back to you. This can cause problems, especially if the document must be turned around in a hurry and the witness is signing on a weekend: during the week, banks are usually good places to find notaries, but typically they're closed on weekends. If you have this problem, two good places where notaries can often be found are car dealerships and bulk mailing outlets for carriers like Federal Express and the United Parcel Service. Even though your witness is not seeking to buy a car or mail a package, the notary should notarize the document. Law firms also usually have notaries on staff. If you know a lawyer in the town where the witness will be signing, you can often arrange for a notary to be available through that lawyer's firm.

b. Declarations

If you're concerned that no notary will be available or you just want to avoid the trouble of getting a document notarized, and if your jurisdiction will allow declarations, then preparing a declaration is often a simpler and more efficient method of warranting the accuracy of information. The form for declarations is usually dictated by rule or statute: in federal court the provision simply requires that a declarant located in the United States sign and date a declaration, under penalty of perjury, that everything in the document is true and correct.[7] The form for a declarant outside of the United States is similar, although not identical.

F. Voir Dire and Jury Instructions

Once a case gets close to trial, courts will often ask the parties to prepare the jury instructions they want the judge to give at the end of trial. Depending on your jurisdiction, you may also be asked to provide the judge with a series of voir dire questions, the questions that allow the parties to uncover any potential jurors who have opinions that are either favorable or unfavorable to them.

These documents present some writing challenges, because they are intended to be read aloud by the judge to the jury (or prospective jury members) and so should sound as natural as possible when read, and yet they must convey some technical legal information which is often couched in sterile, legal language. In terms of formatting, however, they are relatively straightforward.

i. Voir Dire

Many jurisdictions allow the lawyers to question the potential jurors (or "venire," as they're sometimes called) directly. If that's the case

---

7. 28 U.S.C. § 1746.

in your jurisdiction, you likely can ignore this section. But in some courts, the judge will conduct the voir dire process alone, allowing the attorneys—at most—some follow-up questions after hearing a juror's response. In those jurisdictions, the judge will often ask the parties to submit written questions they would like the judge to ask. If you're involved in a case where the judge expects this, the requirements for the questions and the date by which the questions should be submitted will likely be given in a scheduling or pretrial order.

If you're trying the case away from home, be sure an attorney familiar with the jurisdiction tells you what's expected of you when preparing these voir dire questions. For example, you may be tempted to ask questions that are biased in your client's favor. But in most cases, judges won't ask questions exactly as they're written: the judge will likely try to edit out the bias and ask a more balanced question. If you know this beforehand, you may consider whether it would be more effective for your client if you asked questions that appear neutral but which still allow you to discern potential bias from a potential juror.

During the voir dire process, the potential jurors should get a very general sense of what the litigation is about and who the participants at trial will be, and they should have the chance to explain any bias they may have. Typical voir dire questions will ask the potential jurors if they know any of the parties, if they work for any of the parties or if they have a financial stake in the parties (if there's a company or corporation involved), and if they know the attorneys or potential witnesses. If there's a product involved, you will probably want to know if the potential jurors have the same or a similar product at home, or if they have other products manufactured by the party who made the one at issue in the case.

You will likely also want to know if any previous experience with the civil or criminal justice system will make it difficult for any potential juror to render an impartial verdict based on the law and the evidence, if the potential jurors have religious convictions or other preconceived ideas that would make it difficult for them to decide fairly, or if they have any life experiences that might affect them in their deliberations. Sometimes these life experiences may be embarrassing or awkward for the potential jurors to talk about in public. Judges will often group these questions—typically those asking the potential jurors if they or any of their immediate family have been victims of crime, if they've ever been arrested, if they've ever been a party to a lawsuit, and other similar issues—and rather than ask for an immediate answer, they will ask for each person who responds "yes" to approach the bench and discuss the answer in private, with only the judge, attorneys, and (sometimes) the parties able to hear.

The typical form for a series of voir dire questions follows the standard format for filing documents with a court. After the caption and title, the first paragraph should include a very general summation of the claims and defenses of the parties, and each question should have its own numbered paragraph so the judge's failure to ask a specific question, or to ask a question in the form provided by counsel, can be objected to with the question readily identified. After the questions, the document should include a standard signature block and a certificate of service, because the other side will get a copy of your voir dire questions and will likely object to any it feels are too biased.

ii. Jury Instructions

Jury instructions are given to the jury by the judge at the end of the presentation of the evidence and before the jury begins its deliberations. The judge will usually want to see proposed instructions from the parties much sooner, however—often before the trial starts. The judge will usually hold these proposed instructions until the evidence has all been presented and will then hold a hearing while the jury is not in the courtroom to decide which instructions, and in what form, will actually be read to the jury. At this hearing you should have the opportunity to submit supplemental proposed instructions if something unexpected has happened at trial.

Many jurisdictions—federal and state—have pattern jury instructions for the substantive legal questions juries must face. Although these are often poorly drafted, they're usually safe choices because they've been used in numerous jury trials without objection from trial or appellate courts, so their inclusion likely won't cause the jury's verdict to be overturned. And in many jurisdictions, the use of pattern instructions is mandatory if they cover the issue of law at question. There are also some commercial publications containing jury instructions for a variety of situations. As with all commercial form books, you should review such instructions very carefully to be sure they conform to the law in your jurisdiction.

The judge hearing your case might also have some boilerplate language for some of the procedural issues that come up in every trial and about which the jury must be instructed. Such issues—the jury being the judge of the facts, the jury having to listen and apply all the judge's instructions as a whole, and so on—are usually uncontroversial and require little support. The judge or the judge's law clerk should tell you if the judge has such boilerplate instructions. You might also find them in the instructions for earlier trials your firm has had in front of this judge.

If your trial has a substantive issue of law for which there is no pattern instruction, either jurisdiction-specific or commercial, you will have to draft your own instruction. Once you have researched the law, you will need to distill the court or statutory language into something a nonlawyer will understand without changing the meaning of the rule of law you are articulating. After a short while, you will likely have more respect for the drafters of the pattern instructions: turning complex rules of law into easy-to-understand language is a challenging exercise. Although there are no rules for drafting the language of these unique instructions, you should take your cue from the pattern and boilerplate instructions that constitute the rest of the instructions the jury will hear. Ideally, the tone of all the instructions should be the same and the jury should not be able to tell that different instructions were drafted by different people.

Jury instructions usually come with a cover page with the case caption at the top of it and "Plaintiff's (or Defendant's) Jury Instructions" in the center. Each instruction should have its own page with the heading "Plaintiff's (or Defendant's) Proposed Jury Instruction No. ___" in underlined and centered text. On the single-spaced line after the heading, still centered but enclosed in parentheses, you should give a short description of what this instruction is about.

The body of the instruction should come next, in double-spaced text. Although the standard font size for legal documents is 12 points, you might consider typing your instructions in a 14-point font if you think the judge will be reading directly from your proposed instruction.

At the foot of the page, you should cite all sources that contributed to the instruction. If the instruction is taken verbatim from a pattern jury instruction, a citation of the specific instruction is sufficient. If you have changed any of the language, you should indicate that you have amended the pattern instruction. And if you have added to the instruction based on law you found in a case, you should cite both the pattern instruction and the case or cases you used to draft the addition. It's important that you indicate that the instruction has been amended even if only a word has been added or omitted: you don't want to give the judge the impression that you're making subtle changes to pattern instructions without telling anyone.

On the page opposite is an example of a jury-instruction page with the instructions in 14-point font.

Although it may seem wasteful to have such a short instruction taking up one page and although you may be tempted to combine several instructions on one page, you should resist that impulse unless you have specific instructions from the judge to the contrary. The space allows the judge or the judge's law clerk to write in

Plaintiff's Jury Instruction No. 5
(Weight of Testimony)

After you have considered everything concerning the credibility of a witness, you may decide to accept all, some, or none of that witness's testimony. You, and you alone, decide how much credibility and weight, if any, that testimony deserves.

East Dakota Pattern Jury Instruction 9:87 (as amended).

changes to the instructions you submit if necessary or to make other notes on the page. And if the judge decides not to give one of your instructions, that one-page instruction can be removed from the pile of pages without disturbing the other instructions that the judge will give.

G. Appellate Briefs

Appellate briefs are the most heavily formatted of legal documents most lawyers will prepare in their careers. Nothing you'll have to do is especially complicated, but it will take time: you should plan to spend at least one full day assembling the necessary tables, drafting the cover page, and making sure that the other formatting details are correct before submitting your brief.

A word of caution, one I've sounded before but repeat here because it's so important for your well-being. Most senior lawyers, and almost all clients, will not understand how long it takes to put a document like this into final form. Many of the formatting steps discussed here can only be taken after the last edit to the document is made: adding or subtracting text will often change page numbers, for example, so tables of contents and authorities have to be checked at the end of the editing process. But because this work is not substantive in nature, those who are not responsible for getting a complicated document ready for filing often have little understanding of how much time it will take, so they will delay relaying any changes to you until the last possible second. This can leave you with very little time to get the document ready to be filed. For your own self-protection, you should plan for the possibility that the last day, and certainly the last few hours, before the brief is filed will be hectic.

The best step you can take to prepare yourself for filing is to develop and follow a checklist of what tasks need to be done and set a deadline for doing them. After you have had some experience, preparing and following a checklist will become less necessary. But for your first few briefs, you should make a complete list of all crucial sections in the brief and all crucial due-dates, ending, of course, with the filing deadline. Having a written reminder of what needs to be in the brief and when it needs to be filed should reduce your stress somewhat.

With all this in mind, let's look at the various parts of a standard appellate brief and how to format them. Bear in mind that each jurisdiction has its own rules for how documents should be presented and what should be in them. If your jurisdiction's rules differ from the advice given here, those rules must control what you write and how you present it. And if your jurisdiction has rules about what a brief must contain, you should add these rules to your checklist to make sure you take care of them.

i. Cover Page

This serves essentially the same function as the caption on a trial brief, but it takes up more space and is formatted differently. Appellate courts typically require litigants to prepare their cover pages in different-colored paper. In federal court, for example, cover pages must be blue for appellant, red for appellee, green for *amici* or intervenors, and gray for a reply brief.[8]

The elements of an appellate cover page are as follows:

- court name—single-spaced, centered, bold-faced, and capitalized; be very careful here: the court name is the name of the court in which the appeal will be heard, not the court from which the appeal is being taken;

- at least one double space and a two-inch line;

- appellant's name—centered and capitalized, and followed by a comma; this is followed by a single space and a description of the appellant's roles in both the lower and appellate courts ("Defendant—Appellant," for example);

---

8. Fed. R. App. P. 32(a)(2).

- a double space, then a "v.";

- another double space, then the appellee's name—centered and capitalized, and followed by a comma; this is followed by a single space and a description of the appellee's roles in both the lower and appellate courts ("Plaintiff—Appellee," for example);

- at least one double space, then the lower court information; for example: "On Appeal From The Circuit Court For Fictitious County"; this should be centered and have initial capital letters;

- at least one double space and a three-inch line;

- one double space, then the name of the document; for example, "brief of plaintiff-appellee Global Oil Company"; this should be bold-faced, centered, and typed in all capital letters; it should also be single-spaced if it extends beyond one line;

- at least one double space and another three-inch line;

- at least one double space, then the names of the attorney filing the brief, together with address and telephone numbers, aligned at the right margin and single-spaced;

- one double space, then a description of whom the attorney represents; for example, "Attorney for Plaintiff-Appellee Global Oil Company";

- one double space, then the date—aligned at the left margin—and the words "oral argument requested" (if you want an oral argument; note, though, that this isn't always the case: don't ask for an oral argument unless you've thought about it and really want one), all capitalized and centered on the page; because you already have text on this line, the automatic page centering feature of your word processor won't work here, so you'll have to use the tabs to put this text in the center: one or two tabs should move the text over sufficiently so that it's centered;

- one double space, then a double line running from the left margin to the right margin; your word processor should be able to insert such a line automatically (in Microsoft Word, for example, type "Control+Shift+D," then tab across the page).

All of these elements may seem complicated, but they're simple once you see the result. The only complication is the indeterminacy of some of the spacing . This can occur because the information on a cover page should fit onto one page and the more information that's required, the less space there will be between the various elements of the page. So once you have the elements of the cover page assembled, you may have to tinker with line spacing so that everything fits onto one page and doesn't look either too cramped or too spread out. An example is found on the following page.

Your cover page should not have a page number. This can cause some numbering problems when you assemble your document for final printing. Although there are ways to automate your word processor to number some portions of the document and not others, the simplest solution is to create a separate document for the cover page and suppress page numbering in that document.

ii. Tables

Even if your local jurisdiction doesn't require tables of contents and authorities, a properly formatted appellate brief should include these elements. Formatting suggestions for tables are included in the previous chapter on common elements.

The tables should have page numbers, but they're numbered differently from the body of the text. Again, there are software solutions to this problem, but the simplest practice is to create a third document for the tables. You should set the page numbers in the standard manner—with no number on the first page and the other page numbers centered at the foot of the page. But instead of the

IN THE SUPREME COURT OF
EAST DAKOTA

A.B.C. CORPORATION, INC.,

Defendant—Appellant

v.

GLOBAL OIL COMPANY, et al.,

Plaintiff—Appellee.

On Appeal From The Circuit Court

For Fictitious County

BRIEF OF PLAINTIFF—APPELLEE GLOBAL OIL COMPANY

Polly Peachum
Peachum, McHeath & Lockit, LLP
321 Main Street
Nowhere City
ED 09876

(321) 555-9876 (phone)
(321) 555-6789 (facsimile)
ppeachum@peachum.com

Attorney for
Plaintiff—Appellee
Global Oil Company

July 21, 2005   ORAL ARGUMENT REQUESTED

Arabic numerals you'll use in the body of the brief, you should use lowercase Roman numerals. Your word processing software should be able to format your tables with such numerals without difficulty.

iii. Other Formatting Issues

In drafting the statement of facts for an appellate brief, you must refer to the record established in the lower court. The record, and an extract of the most important documents within the record, will have been submitted to the court and is the source of all the facts you'll be including in your statement of facts. All pages of the record will have been numbered prior to filing, so citing the record is relatively simple. The first time a record reference appears in your brief, cite the full name of the record and then define that name as "R." For example: "Joint Record Extract ("R.") at 4." Note that this is a generic way of referring to the record, appropriate for some courts. Courts and some citation manuals have their own requirements for how attorneys should refer to the record. As always, you should check with the applicable rules for the court in which you will be filing your brief.

The federal appellate rules suggest that briefs be typed in a proportionally spaced serif font of 14-point size or larger.[9] In practice, this usually means Times New Roman font. But be very cautious here: in at least one state court, the rule suggesting the use of Times New Roman font can't be trusted.[10]

The Ohio Supreme Court specifically allows Times New Roman font for briefs.[11] But its formatting rule also requires that the brief have no more than 80 characters per line.[12] Times New Roman will allow 81 characters instead of the 80 required by the rule, and the

---

9. Fed. R. App. P. 32(a)(5).

10. My thanks to Brenda Majdalani for this information and for her permission to share it.

11. Ohio Sup. Ct. Prac. R. VII, Section 4 (A)(3).

12. *Id.*

Ohio Supreme Court's clerks will reject briefs with 81 characters per line, even if they are drafted in the apparently authorized Times New Roman font. So in Ohio, at least, your font choice should be 12-point Arial, because that is a font that meets the state's font requirements but will generate only 80 characters per line.

The moral here is twofold: first, never think that the clerk's office will not strictly enforce formatting requirements that might, to you, seem foolish and arbitrary; and second, even a careful reading of the rules is no substitute for a well-informed and experienced local counsel who knows not only the rules but also how the clerk's office will interpret them.

There's another important quirk to mention, this time related to the federal appellate rules. If you follow the rule to use a 14-point font, the print size will be much larger than you may be used to and you will get fewer words onto the page. You won't really lose anything—briefs formatted in this way are subject to a word count rather than a page count[13]—but that's where the problem lies.

You must certify the number of words contained in your brief in a separate certification by the attorney telling the court how many words are in the brief.[14] If you are using Microsoft Word, the word counter will not count words contained in a footnote unless you specifically tell it to. Therefore, be sure to check the box in the word counter tool marked "include footnotes and endnotes." And don't rely on the good nature of the courts to save you. The Seventh Circuit let one attorney escape sanctions because of a general lack of awareness of this glitch.[15] It's unlikely this will happen again.

Because many sections of the brief are not counted against the word count, a simple counting of the number of words may count more words than necessary, leading to unnecessary cutting. In order to get an accurate word count, you should first use your word

---

13. Fed. R. App. P. 32(a)(7)(B).
14. Fed. R. App. P. 32(a)(7)(c)).
15. *DeSilva v. DiLeonardi*, 185 F.3d 815 (7th Cir. 1999).

processor's word counter, then double-check the result. One way to do this is to make a copy of the brief, paste the copy into a new document, highlight all the words in the text that the rules require to be counted, then check the number of words in the highlighted section. You should not do this with the working draft of your brief in case something disastrous happens and you lose the only copy of your final brief.

Also, you should count the number of words only at the very end of the drafting process, when you are certain that no further changes will be made to the text. If you count earlier, there is a strong possibility that you will forget to recount at the end of the process and the word count will be inaccurate. If you're wondering whether anyone will count the words, the answer is assuredly "yes." If either the court or your opponents think you've attempted to gain an unfair advantage by certifying a fewer number of words than the brief actually contains, either or both will count each word. It doesn't take as long as you may think, and if your opponents catch you with a brief that's too long, they will take great delight in seeking to have your brief stricken. Even if the court denies the request, you'll appear as if you tried to get an unfair advantage and have been caught. This isn't a strong position to be in when you are going into an appeal.

Appellate briefs require some sections that aren't required by trial memoranda. You should check the governing rules in the jurisdiction in which your brief will be filed to be sure of what formatting requirements that court has.

Finally, section headings should typically be capitalized, bold-faced, centered on the page, and underlined. Subheadings and all other formatting elements—page numbers, block quotes, term definitions, signature blocks, and so on—should follow the suggestions contained in the previous chapters.

Chapter 9

Business Correspondence

Business correspondence used to mean only letters, typed on a typewriter and mailed or hand-delivered. The letter was the only recognized form of conveying written information to clients and to other attorneys outside of one's firm. Although this kind of document requires a great deal of formatting, the procedure for preparing it is relatively straightforward and easy to learn.

The advent of the word processor and the Internet means that letters are now even easier to prepare and that much business correspondence is also conducted via e-mail. In addition, the facsimile machine (commonly referred to as the "fax machine") has become a standard feature of law practice. These new forms of transmitting correspondence are convenient but have their own formatting issues. As always, check the local rules—in this case, the standard procedures for your office—to make sure the following suggestions conform to the accepted practices.

A. The Lawyer's Role in Preparing Correspondence

Many law students and lawyers think that learning basic formatting rules for correspondence is below them, a task that is properly the work of secretaries and legal assistants. And it is true that most of a law firm's correspondence is written or dictated by lawyers and the technical details of getting the correspondence ready to be delivered are handled by the support staff.

But as with document formatting questions, you should be very cautious about assuming what is and what is not your job as a lawyer. Put simply, your job is to represent your client to the best of your abilities. That means you will often be at the office when the support staff is not. You should know how to work all the principal office machines—photocopiers, facsimile machines, labeling machines for mail carriers, and so on, and you should be able to format and print your own correspondence. You should never assume that any task in the office is below you.

Law firms generate a high volume of mail during the course of a day, and professional secretaries are often more familiar than attorneys with correspondence conventions. So if you know your secretary to be competent and careful, you may well be able to trust that the correct information will go to the correct people and leave the mechanics of letter-sending to your secretary.

But not all of you will be going to firms with experienced, professional secretaries. Some of you may work without a secretary at all. And even for those of you who do have secretaries, if there's a mistake (for example, the "bcc" recipients' page is inadvertently sent to the wrong people) the blame will come back to you, the letter's sender. All documents that leave an office under your name are your responsibility. You can't, and shouldn't, evade that responsibility by blaming a mistake on your secretary. Even if your secretary sends out your correspondence, it's your responsibility to make sure that everything about it is correct. Delegating that responsibility doesn't absolve you of blame if something goes wrong.

There's another reason you should pay attention to the information in this chapter. If you're in law school or if you're unhappy with your job in practice, you'll almost certainly be thinking about sending out letters applying for jobs. To do so, you'll have to create your own letterhead (unless you go to the trouble and expense of getting engraved stationery), and you'll have to format your own letters as well. Understanding how to create and format your own correspondence will help to create in that correspondence the professional appearance we all strive for when being considered for a job.

B. Letters

Letters have a standardized format that has changed little in the past fifty years. Even though some formatting elements might appear outmoded, or have their origins in the days of typewriters and carbon paper, they are still essential to the appearance of a professionally produced piece of correspondence.

i. Letterhead

The first thing you need to consider is a letterhead. If you're working for a law firm, it will likely have its own letterhead. If you're writing for yourself, however, you'll need to create your own. Technology allows us to create letterheads on the word processor without requiring the purchase of expensive printed or embossed letterhead.

As with all letterheads, the final decision of how it looks is up to you. Here's a relatively conservative example:

PEACHUM, MCHEATH & LOCKIT, LLP

ATTORNEYS AT LAW
321 MAIN STREET
NOWHERE CITY, ED 09876

TELEPHONE (321) 555-9876

FACSIMILE (321) 555-6789

Polly Peachum
DIRECT DIAL NUMBER
(321) 555-4321
E-MAIL:
PPEACHUM@PEACHUM.COM

Your letterhead should be in a different font from that you will use in the body of your letter. This sets up a visual contrast with the text of the letter and allows the reader's eyes to glide directly to the substance of the letter. A good conservative choice for the letterhead is Book Antiqua font. Note also that the font size and emphasis changes to create the letterhead's appearance. In this example, the firm name is in 16-point type, with the name in full capitals and the "LLP" designation in small capitals. The address is in 8-point type. The name of the attorney, Polly Peachum, is in 8-point type, and the remaining information under the name is in 7-point type, although in capital letters.

ii. Preliminary Information

After the letterhead, you should leave at least a double space, then tab over to the three-inch mark and type the date. Use the font and the type size you will use for the body of the letter. Never allow the word processor to fill in the date automatically, and politely encourage anyone who types letters for you to fill in the date manually, not rely on the word processor to do so automatically. If the date is filled in automatically, the word processor will likely provide the current date whenever the document is reopened, not the date on the original document. This can be undesirable if, for example, there is no paper record of the date the letter was sent and you later open the letter in the word processor to check the transmission date.

Once you've typed in the date, double-space, flush left to the margin, and type in the transmission mechanism for the letter, in all capital letters, bold and underlined. For example, if you're sending the letter through the mail, type "via first-class mail"; if you're sending it by facsimile, type "via facsimile"; and if you're sending it by both methods (a common practice, especially when you send a letter to a client who wants the information right away but also wants a copy with your signature for the file), type "via facsimile and first-class mail." Other standard transmission mechanisms indicate express delivery services, such as Federal Express and UPS, and hand delivery.

After entering the transmission mechanism, double-space and type the addressee's name and address. These elements should be set in normal type (usually designated as "roman" or "regular" in most word processors), and they should not be bold-faced, underlined, or capitalized in ways that are out of the ordinary. After typing the name and address, double space (at least), tab one stop; type "Re:"; tab one more stop; and type a brief description of the subject of the letter. This can be the client's file number, the name of the litigation or transaction, or some other very brief description of the letter's subject.

iii. The Body of the Letter

After the preliminary information, the body of the letter begins with the salutation. This should be typed at least one double space from the subject line, should be flush to the left margin, and should always begin "Dear." Depending on how well you know the recipient, you can then type the recipient's first name or title (Mr., Ms., and so on) with last name, and then a colon. If you're in any doubt as to whether you know the recipient well enough to use a first name, use the last name only.

Each subsequent paragraph of the letter body is separated by a double space and a one-tab indent. The body of the letter itself, however, should be single-spaced. If the letter is longer than one page, it should have a running header that contains the name of the recipient, the date of the correspondence, and the page number. Your word processor should be able to insert headers like this with ease. The positioning of page numbers in headers differs from that of page numbers in other documents.

The body of your letter, single-spaced, should make your point in as succinct a fashion as possible. If you're enclosing something with the letter, don't type, "Enclosed, please find...." This is a standard enclosure sentence you will see often, but it has been long-de-rided and is slowly falling out of fashion. It's better to type, simply, "I have enclosed...."

iv. Signing

When you're finished with the body of your letter, double-space, tab to the three-inch mark (aligned with the date), and type, "Very truly yours," followed by a comma. The "v" is capitalized because, technically, it marks the beginning of a new sentence. Also, the comma is appropriate after "yours." Then double-space at least twice (preferably more often) and type your name. The space, of course, gives you room to sign your name once the letter is printed, so it should be large enough to accommodate your handwriting.

In practice, you will often be asked to sign someone else's letter. If you do so, you should first make sure the letter is free of any ty-pographical errors (despite any assurances that the letter is ready to sign) and, to the extent possible, is correct in all other details. Then write out the name of the sender followed by a virgule (backslash) and your initials. This shows the recipient that someone other than the sender signed and sent the letter.

A tip you may find useful is always to sign letters in blue ink. This allows you to distinguish clearly between the original and the black-and-white photocopies of the letter. You should always keep copies of final, signed versions of all letters sent out under your name. Word processor copies of letters you send aren't sufficient, unless they're scanned copies of the signed original.

After the signature, there is still some business to accomplish. If this letter is accompanying an enclosure of any sort, double-space after the printed sender's name and type "encl." to show that there should be at least one document accompanying the letter. Then double-space again and enter the initials of the sender, all in capi-tals, followed by a virgule and the lowercase initials of the typist if they are different from those of the sender.

If the letter was faxed, you should attach to the file copy the fax cover sheets, not only showing that each letter was faxed but also confirming that the fax was received. If there were transmission problems before the document finally went through, you should also attach the transmission sheets indicating the problems. This will save you trouble if, as sometimes happens, you fax a letter to opposing counsel who later claims not to have seen the letter. Of course, you can never prove that someone received a faxed transmission, but being able to show the court a cover sheet indicating the date and time of transmittal and the confirmation of receipt attached to the letter itself will be very persuasive in supporting your argument.

v. Copies

Finally, we must deal with the issue of copies. Let me caution you that in copies of letters most mistakes appear, often with embarrassing consequences for the sender, so pay special attention to this issue. As a lawyer, you want to maintain scrupulous records of not only who receives correspondence but also who receives copies of that correspondence.

If you don't care that the recipient knows who else is receiving a copy of the letter, double-space after the typist information, type "cc:" (for "carbon copy" — a holdover from typewriter days) and, after two spaces, type the other recipient's name. (Of course, type the other names if there are other recipients.) If one recipient (or more) is an attorney, you should type "Esquire" after the name.

If you don't want the recipient to know who's getting the copies, or if it's not relevant for the recipient to have that information, then enter a page break, type in "bcc:" (for "blind carbon copy") and, after two spaces, type the names of the other recipients. These recipients might be, for example, other attorneys who are working on the case and who should be informed about developments, or insurers who are monitoring the work you are doing on a case.

If you don't want the "bcc" recipient to know that someone else is getting a copy of the letter as well, enter another page break, type "dbcc:" (for "double blind carbon copy") and, after two spaces, type the names of the other recipients. It's certainly possible that your letter will have multiple recipients, so you could have several "cc"s, some "bcc"s, and a "dbcc" or two as well. Consequently, each set of blind recipients should appear on a separate page.

So far so good. The problem comes when you copy and mail the letter. You must be very careful that each recipient receives only the level of information you want that recipient to receive. In other words, the recipient of the letter gets only the letter. This will show the "cc" recipients. The "cc" recipients also get only the letter. The "bcc" recipients get the letter *and* the page marked "bcc." The "dbcc" recipients get the letter, the "bcc" page, and the "dbcc" page. And all of this—all pages of the letter and all pages showing various levels of recipients—should be entered into your file in order for you to have a record of exactly who received the letter (with enclosures, if any) and how they received it. Many law firms keep file copies on differently colored paper to show that what's in the file are indeed copies.

On pages 176–77 is a sample letter with a copy being sent to one person and a blind copy being sent to someone else.

C. Facsimile Cover Sheets

Do you really need to know about these? If your employer doesn't have standard cover sheets, you certainly do. Your word processor will likely have several standard cover sheet templates, and these are fine for personal use. But if you're creating a fax cover sheet for your professional use, there are some refinements you'll need.

The first of these is simple: use the letterhead you've created as the heading of your cover sheet. It has all the relevant information and it already looks professional, so it's the best and simplest choice.

Then comes the date. The best choice for a cover sheet is to center the date one double space after the last part of the letterhead. After another double space, but again centered—and this time in all capital letters, bold and underlined—type "telecopy cover sheet." These days, a fax isn't typically referred to as a "telecopy," but that's the correct name for it.

Now comes the confidentiality notice, the most important part of the cover sheet. Errors in transmission aren't that common, but they do happen. If you have confidentiality language on the cover sheet, you have some measure of protection. If you don't, and the fax is sent to the wrong person, then someone who shouldn't have the transmission has it, and you have all sorts of confidentiality and privilege problems to deal with.

This notice should be indented one tab stop at both the left and right margins, and it should be in slightly smaller type than the other language on the cover sheet—10-point Times New Roman is ideal. In order to highlight the important text in the notice—especially since it's in smaller type—you should place it in a text box. Your word processor should allow you to format such a box without difficulty.

After the confidentiality notice, the standard cover sheet information—readily obtained from your word processor's templates—should be added, including spaces for the sender's name and phone number so that, in the event of a miscommunication, the fax can be destroyed or returned. On page 178 is a sample complete cover sheet for your reference. Please note that the confidentiality language here is for demonstration purposes only. You shouldn't rely on the language itself to achieve the desired effect of keeping your faxed information confidential.

PEACHUM, MCHEATH & LOCKIT, LLP

ATTORNEYS AT LAW
321 MAIN STREET
NOWHERE CITY, ED 09876

TELEPHONE (321) 555-9876

FACSIMILE (321) 555-6789

Polly Peachum

DIRECT DIAL NUMBER
(321) 555-4321
E-MAIL:
PPEACHUM@PEACHUM.COM

July 30, 2005

VIA FIRST CLASS MAIL

John Doe
President, Global Oil Company.
654 South Avenue
Nowhere City, ED09876

Re: A.B.C. Service, Inc. v. Global Oil Company

Dear Mr. Doe:

I have enclosed a copy of the transcript of your July 1, 2005 deposition. Please review the transcript carefully and let me know if you believe the court reporter made any mistakes in transcribing your testimony.

Please feel free to call me with any questions you might have.

Very truly yours,

Polly Peachum

encl.
PP/ig
cc: George McHeath Esquire

bcc: John Gay

PEACHUM, MCHEATH & LOCKIT, LLP

ATTORNEYS AT LAW
321 MAIN STREET
NOWHERE CITY, ED 09876

TELEPHONE (321) 555-9876

FACSIMILE (321) 555-6789

Date: July 30, 2005

TELECOPY COVER SHEET

THE FOLLOWING DOCUMENT SHOULD BE DIRECTED TO:

TO: _____   FAX NO: _____

FROM: _____   FILE NO: _____

COMMENTS:

NUMBER OF PAGES: _____ (INCLUDING COVER SHEET)

PLEASE CALL IF THIS TRANSMISSION IS INCOMPLETE OR ILLEGIBLE.

SENDER'S NAME: _____ SENDER'S NUMBER: _____

D. E-mail

It's become a cliché to say that the advent of the Internet has brought about a communication revolution, but it's also true. And one of the problems with revolutions is that rules governing conduct can be difficult to discern. That's the case with e-mails, especially in the context of legal writing.

The informality of this form of communication can easily lead one into forgetting that it serves essentially the same function as every document a lawyer writes—conveying information in written form. So although the appearance and transmission mechanism might be different, the fundamental rules for e-mails are the same as for all other documents you prepare. Professional e-mails should be written in grammatically correct, noncolloquial, plain English, and should be written with the understanding that they might be stored and produced later for a variety of purposes.

Most important, before being sent, they should be edited and proofread, and checked for spelling and content. In short, don't write anything in an e-mail that you wouldn't write in a letter or other more seemingly formal document. And don't write anything in any legal document you wouldn't want to hear read in court.

i.   E-mail Address

The first thing to consider concerning e-mail is your e-mail address. If you work for a law firm, your professional e-mail address will likely be provided for you. But if you're a law student, you might have one or more personal e-mail addresses. This is the address you'll be putting at the top of your resume and application letters, so ask yourself if it conveys the professional image you want to project to potential employers. Addresses like "borntoparty@internetprovider.com" might be fun, and might even be true, but they're not likely to inspire a future employer with confidence about your judgment or your commitment to work.

So if you have an e-mail address that is lifestyle oriented, consider opening up another e-mail account with a simple (or boring) address that you can put on a resume and cover letter without reservation. And if it's a special account set up just for employment purposes, remember to check it periodically to see if you have any messages.

ii. E-mail Basics

When sending an e-mail, you should carefully consider the recipients, just as in a letter. Questions of privilege and work product are the same for e-mails as they are for correspondence. Don't let the informality of the medium lull you into making a privilege mistake you may later regret.

The lesson here is that you must think carefully about who is receiving every communication you send—either formally or, as in e-mails, less formally—and what the implications of the receipt of each document are. You shouldn't fall into the habit of sending letters, copies of letters, or e-mails indiscriminately.

A big trap for e-mail users is the "reply" function. E-mails sent to a large number of recipients might be perfectly benign, but if you draft an e-mail response that you don't want every recipient of the original e-mail to see and you accidentally hit the "reply to all" button (or if the sender was a listserv and you simply hit "reply"), you will likely regret the result. Almost everyone who uses e-mail has had the experience of writing to one person but sending the message to additional, unintended, recipients. If you haven't had this experience, try to avoid having it for the first time at work.

There are a couple of things you can do to protect yourself from this problem. The most extreme method is to never hit the "reply" button in response to an e-mail. Rather, send your reply as a new e-mail, typing only the original sender's e-mail address. Double check that you are sending the message to an individual, not a group or list. A less extreme version of this technique is to never hit the "reply to all" button.

But the best and most secure technique is to never do anything automatically or reflexively. Think about what you're doing, check everything at least once, and edit and proofread every element of an e-mail just as you would any other legal document. These cautions are the safest approach to take and should minimize the danger of making a transmission error.

As a protection, each of your work e-mails should have a signature that contains a modified version of your fax cover sheet's confidentiality language, as well as your contact information. It's always good to give recipients your address, phone number, and fax number in case they want to reply to your e-mail in different ways. And although the confidentiality language may not be much of a defense in a case of mistransmission, at least it shows that you tried to be careful and have thought about the problems associated with e-mail.

As with paper correspondence, you should save and file all case-related e-mails you receive. This means printing copies of these e-mails and putting them in the paper correspondence file (until your firm becomes a paperless office). You should also store all e-mails electronically in clearly labeled folders on your computer's hard drive. You should also make sure that your e-mail program automatically saves all e-mails you send, and you should print and file copies of these e-mails as well.

If you use some other method of checking and sending e-mails—from a portable device, for example, or from your home computer—be sure to copy any work-related e-mails you send to your office e-mail address. That way, you will have a permanent record of all correspondence sent under your name. If you don't follow this method, your correspondence file will be incomplete and that's something that should never happen.

Finally, never, under any circumstances, use an "emoticon," those typographical expressions of emotion that attempt to be graphical representations of facial expressions. Also avoid the use of e-mail abbreviations such as "IMO" for "in my opinion." As lawyers, you should write in English, using English words, not symbols, abbreviations, or code. So despite what you may do in your personal e-mails, in business-related communications, including e-mails, use only language and words.

Chapter 10

Editing Your Work

You've chosen the words that best express your reasoning and formatted your document in an appropriate way. Now all that's left to do is to edit: and nothing is more important to your work than the editing process.

You might instinctively want to challenge that statement. Surely the research you've conducted, the analysis you've conceived, and the words you've selected to express that analysis are all more important than editing your work after it's been drafted. But as any experienced writer will tell you, editing is at least as important as the research, analysis, and drafting stages of the writing process. Through editing, mistakes are removed, analysis is clarified, and arguments are honed. It's a process you should take very seriously.

Although I've spoken of editing as if it were one process, in fact there are several stages to it. You edit for content, for persuasiveness, for punctuation, for spelling, for grammar, for tone, for citation accuracy, and for form at least, and you should perform each of these kinds of edits several times before turning your work in. As you grow to be more sophisticated editors—particularly editors of your own work—you can perform several of these editing operations at the same time. But for less experienced legal writers, I'd recommend performing each editing operation separately. This will take more time, but it will be time well spent. Your work will be more polished as a result.

Many practitioners will say that this recommendation is all very well, and in an ideal world they would edit this extensively. But the pressure of work is so great and the emphasis on billing time is so extreme that there simply isn't enough time to fine-tune writing to the degree I'm suggesting. To which the only response is that sometimes you have to make sacrifices in order to produce high-quality work. If the client won't pay for the editing process (and many clients will take this short-sighted position), you need to edit on your own time. Both your client and your supervising attorney will expect you to produce excellent work. Without careful attention to the editing process, you will fail to meet those expectations.

A. Beginning the Editing Process

It's important not to start editing too early or too late. If you start too early, you run the risk of cramping your writing; if you start too late, you won't have enough time to edit your work before turning it in. And you have to learn your own "right time" to start editing. Every writer works at a different pace, so it's only possible to give some very general suggestions about the time the editing process should begin.

First, you have to draft, and you need to draft without interference from the editing part of your brain. Nothing creates writer's block (and yes, lawyers suffer from this as much as fiction writers) faster than your brain criticizing every word you write, every concept you express, and every creative decision you make. So you should generate your first draft, if possible, entirely without critical input.

Although it seems like a time-consuming idea, you may want to write the first drafts of your document in longhand. There's no backspace key you can use to erase a word, a line, or a paragraph, so longhand can stop you from being too critical in the drafting process. When you draft at the keyboard, you may find yourself typing the same paragraph—many times word for word—a second or even a third time because your critical side has kicked in and decided it doesn't like what you've written, only to realize five minutes later that the deleted passage is exactly what you needed. I'm not encouraging you to follow such an old-fashioned idea as writing something out by hand, but if you find yourself editing your work as you draft it, using longhand may be one way (among many others) to stop yourself.

Many practicing lawyers will dictate their work and have someone on the support staff type it up for later review. But I strongly urge you to resist the temptation to do this if at all possible (although sometimes time pressure or law firm culture make dictation a necessity). The written product of dictation is nearly always inferior to work that was originally conceived as writing. For many, the writing process allows them to grapple with the analysis at a more fundamental level than spoken thought, which tends to be more superficial. Even those who benefit from talking out their ideas should talk first and then write, rather than talking only into a microphone. Reducing thought to writing involves a discipline that itself can help to trigger thoughts you may otherwise miss.

While dictating is often justified as a time-saving alternative to writing, I don't believe it. The editing and polishing necessary to transform dictated work into clear, coherent, written prose is so much greater than it is for work originally conceived as writing that the total time expended on both dictating and writing is likely about the same.

Once you have a draft on paper, you should read it with a very critical eye. We're very tolerant with our own work, perhaps because we know how much effort we've put into it. You must fight this tendency and be ruthless: if an argument doesn't work, don't talk yourself into leaving it in because it cost you sleepless nights to research and draft it. You must learn to edit your work with the eyes of the reader, not the writer. If arguments don't work, or aren't in the right place, you have to cut them, transfer them to a position somewhere else in the document, or do whatever else it takes to turn in what you believe to be your best work. Be ruthless. If in doubt, cut.

And when I say "draft on paper," I'm speaking literally, not figuratively. Attempting to edit your work on the computer screen is almost always a bad idea. Although you may be successful in making later edits directly onto the electronic version of your document, you should make the first-level edits on a printout of your draft.

Mistakes are easier to catch, formatting glitches are clearer, and second thoughts are easier to implement when you have the printed version of the document in front of you.

There's another practical reason for editing your work on paper. All too often, upon reflection you find you've been too harsh on yourself and the page you've hacked out of your analysis is savable, at least in part. You'll often realize this at the time you type in your editing changes, and you can save a lot of frustration if you haven't simply erased some of your work after you first evaluated it.

In any case, you should save all drafts of your work so you can restore a paragraph that didn't survive the first edit but that appears after the fourth edit to be just what you need. One efficient way to do this is to create a separate document for each editing stage and title the document appropriately. You may want to title the files "Memo re X January 1 Draft," "Memo re X January 2 Draft," and so on. You may also want to include a header or footer with this sort of title so that all those who read the document know which version they're reading.

You should give yourself some time before cutting your work to shreds. Ideally, you should allow two days between the end of the drafting process and the beginning of editing. Two days may be unrealistic, especially if you have a lot of work to do, but you should give yourself at least an evening to refresh your mind before beginning to edit.

B. How to Edit

Ideally, you should edit your work in a quiet place, away from distractions like telephones, e-mails, and office visitors. That can be difficult to accomplish, especially in a law firm. But even in that busy environment, there are usually some places—empty offices, library tables, and so on—where you can achieve some peace and quiet.

If you must work in your office, close the door to discourage visitors and minimize distractions, don't check your e-mail (try to work somewhere where you can't even see your computer screen), and don't answer the phone. You may have to wait until after normal business hours until things settle down enough to allow you to edit your work in peace. But whenever you do edit, try to find some quiet time when, undisturbed, you can devote your energy solely to the editing process: your work will be better if you can.

Once you begin editing, you should go about the process methodically. You should develop a checklist of different edits and go through the list one item at a time, concentrating on the item at hand to the exclusion of all others: don't make a spelling change if you're not at the spelling-editing stage yet; don't correct a citation error if you haven't yet reached the stage for citation edits; and so on. You don't want to become distracted by looking for too many errors at once, and if you're trying to spot and correct all mistakes at the same time, the chances are that you'll miss some of them. If the spelling mistake or the citation error was obvious, you'll catch it later.

The one exception to this suggestion is that if you've already performed an editing stage (say for spelling errors) and later find a spelling mistake, you should correct the mistake. This shouldn't happen often, and if it does happen, you should take it as a warning that your editing skills need some work. You should also plan to do another complete spelling edit before turning the document in.

Once you've edited everything on paper, type your changes (thinking about each one before you type it), then edit the next draft. Economics and time efficiency may require you to give your work to someone else, like a secretary, to make the changes to the document. Try hard to resist this. Making your own edits, and those of others if others are editing the document as well, can stimulate your brain to rethink what's been drafted and can be a very productive time.

While you've been editing, you'll likely have found that you need to go back and do more research to nail down a part of your analysis, or that you need to entirely rework a portion of your document. So there are plenty of opportunities to make mistakes in all the different editing categories, and so you shouldn't omit, for example, a final spelling edit because you checked the spelling on the last round of changes and all the words seemed spelled correctly.

You should continue editing until you run out of things to change. Never leave the editing process after typing a round of changes. Once you've typed changes, edit again. At least you'll be making sure you typed the changes accurately, and at most you'll find another weak spot requiring additional work. But you should only stop editing when you have nothing left to edit.

C. Check Spelling Manually as well as Electronically

Spelling is one of the harder elements of our work to edit because most of us, if we're honest, don't spell as well as we should and the word processor will check our spelling automatically. But even with the benefit of electronic spellchecking, there are at least four different reasons why we should perform manual spelling checks.

First, as you've likely experienced, the word processor doesn't always catch your spelling mistakes. If you intend to type "while" but mistakenly type "whale," the computer will pass over the mistake because "whale" is a word and it's correctly spelled. But it's still the wrong word in context, and only a manual spelling check will tell you that.

Second, editing for spelling forces you to go through your document another time with a very specific, technical goal in mind. Strangely, during this careful, technical rereading, good ideas about the structure of the analysis pop into your mind. The concentration on one element seems to free your mind so it can fix other problems with little conscious thought.

Third, you won't always have access to a spell-checker, and checking spelling manually is a good way to improve your spelling overall. A lawyer who uses a marker and a large sheet of paper to outline the principal points of a case to a jury during trial will lose a lot of credibility if the words on the paper are misspelled.

Fourth, checking your spelling manually will force you to buy and use a good dictionary. Although there are good dictionaries available free online, and you should certainly have at least one good online dictionary bookmarked on the browser of the computer you use to draft your work, you should also have a good dictionary sitting in the place where you edit (and where you draft, if that's a different place). There's no substitute for a good dictionary to be sure that you've used and spelled a word correctly.

None of this is to say that you shouldn't use the spell-checking function on your word processor. On the contrary, you *must* use the spell-checker during every round of the editing process. But you can't rely only on the spell-checker, and therefore you must check your spelling manually as well. It might be tedious and slow, but it's a process that will pay dividends in the end.

D. Techniques to Improve the Editing Process

Suppose you've done everything I've recommended: you've taken your work through five separate drafts and proofread it carefully, and it still comes back from your teacher or supervisor with proofreading mistakes flagged for you. This should be a warning to you that you're still not being careful enough and that your eye is gliding over your mistakes.

One of the problems with editing is our ability to fool ourselves. By this, I mean the mind's incredible ability to see the flaws in someone else's writing with great ease while being incapable of seeing an egregiously misspelled word in the first sentence of one's own document, despite the number of times one reviews it.

There are steps you can take to slow yourself enough to catch the major problems. Some of them might seem foolish, childish, or even humiliating. But don't let ego stand in your way. You don't have an audience for the editing process and you don't have to tell anyone what you did to edit your work. All that's important is the work's quality when it's submitted. With that in mind, think about trying one or more of these ideas:

- Put a ruler under the line you're working on to focus your eyes on one line at a time;

- read your work aloud and slowly (this can be especially helpful in catching problems in tone, disagreement between singular and plural, and tense agreement problems);

- read sections, or even paragraphs, of your work out of order (this can force you to concentrate on the meaning of each unit of your work and can catch logical flaws; it won't help you decide whether you've drafted clear connections between your paragraphs or your sections, though, so if you read for logical flaws, you'll have to combine the technique with an edit specifically to check for smooth transitions);

- read your work backwards—both starting at the end of a line and reading from right to left and starting at the bottom of a page and reading from bottom to top; this technique can help you focus on spelling and on the meaning of each specific word, although it won't help you with problems of flow, so you'll have to combine the technique with a special edit for flow;

- read your work upside down (if all the techniques cited above fail, this one will force you to slow down and think about each word because you won't be able to read it otherwise; I know of several successful lawyers who were forced to do this in front of a senior partner for whom they worked in order to impose on them the importance of accurate proofreading and editing).

E. An Editing Checklist

Here is a sample editing checklist that outlines some of the writing mistakes you might make when drafting a document. Each of us is different, though, and we all have our own special mistakes that crop up time and again in our writing. You should take this checklist and add to it a list of mistakes you, or others, find in your work. Identifying your own writing weaknesses can be painful, but it's the first step to fixing them.

Editing Checklist

1. Electronic Spell Check _____
2. Manual Spell Check _____
3. Citations in Appropriate Form _____
4. Jurisdiction Specific Formatting Requirements _____
5. Subheadings Informative or Argumentative _____
6. Throat Clearing Eliminated _____
7. Passive Voice Use Justified _____
8. Sexist Language Eliminated _____
9. Legalisms and Wordiness Eliminated _____
10. Plain English Used Throughout _____
11. Punctuation Use Correct _____
12. Sentence and Paragraph Length Appropriate _____
13. Agreement between Singular and Plural Checked _____
14. Past Tense When Writing about Cases _____
15. Analysis Organized Coherently _____
16. Writing Flows Well _____
17. Connections between Paragraphs Where Possible _____
18. All Accompanying Documents Drafted _____

F. Finishing the Editing Process

As you're reading this, you may imagine that the editing process is eternal, continuing without end. But legal writers work under deadlines that must be met, and there comes a time when we must stop editing, get the document into final form, and file it—with the court, with a supervising attorney, or with a writing teacher.

Knowing when you are done, of course, is something that comes with time and experience, and everyone has a different perspective on the end of the editing process. I can only offer you my own advice on this. When I know I've spent a considerable time on editing, when I've taken all or most of the steps I've outlined here, when I'm not finding any more mistakes, when I'm satisfied with the thrust of the writing, and—most importantly—when I'm so sick of the project that I can't bear to read another word, then I know I've reached the penultimate edit. After giving myself a break, I have to force myself to go through the document one last time. If, on that reading, I don't change anything, then I'm done. If I do make changes, then I read the document through again and again until I don't make a change, and then I stop.

Once the document is finished, signed, and out the door, prepare yourself for the urge to somehow retrieve it and make some additional changes. You almost certainly can't get to your document at this point: it's illegal to reach into the mail slot and try to take it back, and courts won't give you the document from the court file once it's been accepted and stamped in. And even if you could get to the document again, the changes you would want to make almost certainly wouldn't improve it.

You should also try hard not to reread the document you've just submitted. Even if you find a mistake on the first page, it's not possible to correct it and all you'll do is make yourself feel incompetent because you know you've filed an imperfect document. Once the document is out of your control, try to forget it and move on with your next assignment. You must let go of your work now and let it do its job.

If you find this difficult, try to remember this: perfection, at least in the realm of legal writing, is an illusion. Even if every word is correctly spelled, every sentence is grammatically correct, every punctuation mark correctly applied, and every component of the analysis has been thought through exhaustively, there will always be a tweak you could make to the argument, a refinement that could ratchet up your client's chances of success. There simply is no such thing as the perfect document.

All you're responsible for is doing your best. If you've researched and written as carefully as you can, and edited and proofread as thoroughly as possible, you've done your best work. You might win, you might not, you might get an "A," you might not: but you can't do any more.

So relax and move on. There are always more documents to write.

Index